A True Story of Bad Things

By July Waters

Copyright © 2024 by July Waters

All rights reserved.

No part of this publication may be reproduced, distributed, or transmitted in any form or by any means, including photocopying, recording, or other electronic or mechanical methods, without the prior written permission of the author or publisher, except as permitted by U.S. copyright law.

For privacy reasons, some names, locations, and dates may have been changed. No identification with actual persons (living or deceased), places, buildings, and products is intended or should be inferred.

Second edition 2024

Table of Contents

~~Happily~~ Married	1
When They Were Young	2
Betrothed	9
Wedding Day	12
Honeymoon Disappointments	16
Don't Pay the Bills	22
Yes, Master	25
Kiss Me Not	28
Shut Your Mouth	33
You're Not a Looker, Beth	35
Bedroom Bond	38
Beth Needs a Hug	43
To Pee or Not to Pee	45
Bringing Down the House	49
Things Get Physical	53
Road Trip	56
Beth Fights an Intruder	59
The Devil is Coming	66
Mark Ditches Construction	69

Mark's Shopping Spree	73
Push-Mowing Her Life Away	76
Lone Wolf	81
Playing Pool at the Bar	87
Chimichanga	90
The Truth Came Out of the Closet	99
Ride or Die to Memphis	101
Ready, Aim...	104
Vacation Time	107
Family Photo	116
Rage Drive	118
Worth a Thousand Words	124
Oil Change	126
Dust and Deer Lanes	130
Deadbeat	134
Perpetually Late	140
Days and Hours	145
Gaslighting	147
Lies, Lies, Lies	152
Mark the Narc	157
College Days	160

Four-Wheeler	165
Empty Nest	169
No Good Memories	171
Sex Schedule	172
Deer Hunting Comes First	177
Ordered to Cheat	180
A Time for Truth	181
Like a Puppet on a String	183
An Apology for the Records	189
Apology, Null and Void	194
Hitting Rock Bottom	199
Passport	202
Jake	206
Falling in Love	212
A Friend in the Fire	214
A Time for Lies	217
Final Chapter- It's Just the Beginning	221

Prologue

The changes were subtle. In the beginning, she wore bright colors and bold prints. She was full of life, and it showed.

Then one day she looked across the sea of clothing in her closet and realized there were no pretty colors in her wardrobe anymore. Everything she owned was gray.

It helped her blend in.

It helped her disappear.

~~Happily~~ Married

She'd been married for 25 years and had never once thought of cheating. 25 years of being a loving wife. 25 years of raising children, preparing meals, cleaning the house, mowing the lawn, and working at various jobs.

25 years of being talked to like trash and having her husband's affection withheld from her. 25 years of being told he's not in the mood. 25 years of being told she's not good enough.

In all those 25 years, she never dreamed of stepping outside of the marriage to get her emotional and physical needs met.

Until 25 years and day one.

When They Were Young

Beth's childhood was perfect. She had a mom and dad who loved her, and a brother to ride bikes with. Her Arkansas summers involved endless hours of outdoor play, like swinging on the burlap bag swing Daddy had hung from the great sugarberry tree in the front yard. She loved to swing in the cool breeze of its shady branches.

In the wintertime, she and her brother eagerly awaited the season's first snow. Some years there was no snow, but other years saw some flakes. When they were fortunate enough to get a layer on the ground, they'd often venture into the woods to explore. Everything looked so different when snow was on the ground. They'd search for animal tracks in the snow, and they'd build forts out of boards and tree branches.

Her family did farm life on a small scale. Over the course of her childhood, Beth's family had about 30 head of cattle, a couple of incredibly annoying pigs, a horse or two, and angus steers she and her brother showed in annual competitions. During the summer months, they grew produce to sell. Farm life kept them busy and satisfied.

Beth and her brother spent hour after hour playing in the barn. It was stacked high with bales of hay, and they would often climb and scamper over the bales up to the barn's rafters. Beth was always too afraid to jump from the uppermost parts of the stack, but her brother was brave and took flying leaps from the top down to the dirt floor of the barn. When they weren't climbing on the hay, they were searching the barn for mice nests. They'd often find little nests filled with baby mice. They'd watch them for a while, and then, being farm kids, they'd call to their barn cat to come over and handle business.

Her days on the farm were an endless adventure for Beth. She loved her country life. It's the kind of childhood many children never experience. Her days were filled with chores, sunshine, puppies, livestock, and every kind of outdoor play imaginable.

She also had a love of reading that began to develop when she was no bigger than a baby. Her mother read story after story to her and her brother, letting the kids sit on her lap and turn the pages of the books. An open book was an invitation to adventure, adventures that she enjoyed quite often.

Her life was multi-faceted and perfect. She was a rough and tumble kind of girl who loved being outdoors and getting dirty, but she could also be very much a girlie girl who slathered on lipstick and played dress-up. Her bedroom was full of dolls, stuffed animals, and a piano she practiced with her mother's encouragement.

Beth enjoyed her simple, perfect life.

Mark's childhood, on the other hand, was very different. He grew up without a dad. His mom was his caregiver and provider, but she didn't put much effort into either. He was neglected, talked down to, and left to his own devices.

He did see some happy moments in his formative years, but overall, his childhood was lacking. He was made to feel as though nobody loved him. He simply existed.

Beth's childhood was like a dream.

Mark's was a nightmare.

Beth and Mark met in high school. They were nothing more than acquaintances, but Beth found him to be a vulgar, crude, loud boy.

"Hey, look what I can do with this banana," he said at lunch break. He put the tip of it in his mouth, twisted it, and used his tongue and teeth to sculpt it into an accurate replica of a male body part. The other teens laughed, but Beth thought he was the most disgusting person on the face of the planet.

Mark was a redneck rebel type. He sported a mullet, mustache, and most days a faded denim jacket and cowboy boots. He hung out with the misfits, smoked cigarettes, and got drunk on weekends.

Beth couldn't stand him. She was a good girl, a bit of a prude. He was everything she wasn't. They were like oil and water.

Then high school ended, it was gone for good. Beth forgot all about that loud redneck she loathed so much. She set about enjoying the summer before her first semester of college.

She was friends with Mark's younger sister. One bright summer day Beth decided to give her a call. Mark answered the phone.

"This is Beth. Is your sister available?"

"No," he responded. "She won't be home until sometime later this weekend."

"Ok, I'll call back another time. Bye...," Beth said.

"Wait... what are you up to tonight?" Mark quickly asked.

"I'm staying home watching TV," she said.

He slyly responded, "You aren't going out tonight? Don't you have a boyfriend?"

"No, I don't have a boyfriend. I haven't even been on a date in three months," she said.

"That's a shame. If I were your boyfriend, I'd sure take you out to do something fun tonight," he responded.

"Oh?" Beth asked. "What would we do?"

"Well, I'm planning to go to my friend's house and play board games with him and his girlfriend," he said.

"That sounds like fun."

"Maybe you could go with me. I could pick you up at 7:00, Baby Doll," he slyly said.

"Maybe… let me go ask my mom," Beth responded.

After a few months of staying home on weekends, Beth was ready to go out and do something different. She ran to the living room where her mother was watching TV.

"Momma, can I go out with my friend's brother tonight?" she asked. "He's going to his friend's house to play board games."

"I guess it's alright. Just be home by 11:00," her mom told her.

Beth ran back to her bedroom and grabbed her phone. She gave herself a few seconds to slow her breathing, and then she responded to Mark.

"Hey, I can go with you tonight. I'll be ready at 7:00," she told him.

The conversation continued between 18-year-old Beth and 19-year-old Mark. The longer they talked, the more she forgot how much she once despised this boy, and, instead, started to become enamored with him. It was the most innocent thing in the world, a simple phone call. They had no way of knowing it in that moment, but they had embarked on a journey they would share for the next three decades.

Beth was excited about this budding romance. Excited that Mark was interested in her. Excited to be wanted.

She had no clue she had taken the first step on a path that would destroy her mind, heart and soul.

Betrothed

Beth and Mark knew right away they wanted to be married. They started dating in June and got engaged in November. He proposed on a Saturday. The weather was quite cold that day, the trees heavily clad in crystalline ice, the sun brightly shining making the icy branches dance with sparkles. He drove her to the top of the mountain where a state park was located. They walked around enjoying beautiful views of the valley below. And finally, as they stood atop a large rock outcropping, he popped the question. Of course, she said yes.

He didn't have an engagement ring to give her, but somehow she didn't find that to be odd. She wasn't a fancy person, and she wasn't into diamonds, so it really didn't faze her at all.

It bothered her a little that he didn't get down on one knee to propose. He just stood facing her and asked her. But that was no biggie. Or at least she didn't put much thought into it. She was just so happy to be engaged!

When they left the rock outcropping, they drove to the park gift shop. Beth was absolutely beaming with joy as they browsed the gift selection. They came across some horseshoe nails that had been fashioned into rings. Beth found one that fit her ring finger and Mark bought it for the price of 99 cents. Now she had an engagement ring to go with the prior proposal.

Mark said, "I should get down on one knee and propose to you so all the people working in the gift shop will have something to talk about."

"That would be kind of funny," she said, "but I'm super shy and I wouldn't want everyone looking at me."

An outsider with more life experience than what Beth had might look at their proposal story and see a hint of red flags. Maybe a lack of care on Mark's part. Maybe a need for grandiosity when around other people. But Beth didn't see these things. She was so happy to be engaged that no negative possibilities could make their way into her field of vision.

She was as purely and simply happy as she could be. Being scooped up by her own version of a knight in shining armor is something she'd dreamed of since childhood. And here he was. This boy who wanted her. This boy who asked her to be his wife. She was wanted. He had claimed her. And she was happy to accept.

Wedding Day

On a warm summer day the following year, a small group of family and friends gathered in the yard of Beth's family home. She and Mark scheduled their outdoor wedding for dawn. New day, new beginning. Few people were present for the ceremony at such an early hour, but that didn't matter. All that mattered was having the ceremony and becoming husband and wife.

As Beth stood in her mother's bedroom getting dressed for the ceremony, she caught a glimpse of Mark as he walked across the yard. Her heart fluttered. He looked so handsome in his tux. She was ridiculously excited to be marrying this man.

When time for the ceremony neared, Beth stood just inside the doorway of her parents' home, with her arm gently intertwined with her Daddy's. He was about to walk her down the aisle.

She heard the wedding music begin to play.

"Wait," she whispered. "I don't want to do this. I don't want to do this!"

As her entire life flashed before her eyes, she panicked.

"Oh, God! What am I doing?!" she whispered to herself.

Tears streamed down her cheeks. She tried to calm her breathing. She assured herself this was the cold-feet scenario she had heard about, when a bride is suddenly terrified of giving herself to a husband, of giving her life away.

Her beautiful, simple life.

She took a moment to steel her nerves, and as her life continued to flash before her eyes, she walked out the door on the arm of her father. She quietly marched down the aisle to stand beside her soon-to-be husband.

The wedding was simple. Decorations were few, just a couple of floral arrangements on pedestals beside the preacher. Beth's dress had been lovingly handmade by her mother.

She carried a bouquet of artificial flowers in shades of blue and white.

Beth and Mark had purchased simple wedding bands at a reasonable price. All in all, the wedding cost around $400. It was simple and lovely.

As the couple stood before the preacher, the neighbor across the gravel road began plowing his garden. He was working his land the old-fashioned way, with a horse and antique plow. It was quite a sight as Beth and Mark pledged their love for one another in that beautiful, country setting.

Once the ceremony ended and refreshments had been enjoyed, the newlywed couple hit the road for their honeymoon.

The moment before their departure, Mark secretly spoke with Beth's brother.

"Now that I'm married, it's going to be all about me," he confided in hushed tones.

Her brother didn't know how to respond, so he stood stoically quiet. What could he say? This was his sister's wedding day.

Beth had no idea that's what her new husband was thinking only moments after the preacher signed the marriage certificate.

Beth was enraptured with thoughts of, "Now, it's all about us and the life we can build together!"

Mark was thinking, "Now that I'm married, it's all about me and the life I can build for myself."

Beth had no clue.

Honeymoon Disappointments

The couple spent their honeymoon in a cabin near one of Arkansas's most popular trout-fishing streams. Beth had never been to this area of the state before, so Mark started giving her a tour as soon as they arrived. This part of Arkansas was special to him and his family. They had spent a lot of time camping and fishing in the area. The first stop on the tour was a local campground. As they slowly drove through the campground, they saw his grandparents. They were camping there.

"How did they get here before us?? We were all at the same wedding," Beth laughed.

Her second thought was, "We're honeymooning with his grandparents. How weird is that?"

They stopped and visited with Mark's grandparents for a couple of hours. Then they resumed their tour of the area and found a place to eat.

It was a cute little sandwich shop. And because they were on their honeymoon, everything seemed new and exciting, so that made the sandwich shop seem even cuter to Beth.

Mark ordered a footlong sub packed with different kinds of cold cuts and cheese. Beth ordered a pasta dish. The food was delicious!

"Can I have a bite of your sandwich?" Beth asked. "I'll give you some of my pasta."

It seemed like a natural thing to ask her husband, and it definitely seemed like a fair trade. She swallowed the bite she had been working on, paused in expectation, and waited for Mark to pass his sandwich to her. Such a romantic sandwich shop, and such a romantic way to share their first meal. She was absolutely aglow with love for Mark and excitement for their marriage.

"Nope," Mark replied. "You've got your own food. This is mine."

His response stung. She thought couples naturally shared everything. The idea that he would tell her no never crossed her love-stricken mind.

Beth was shocked into silence. As she absorbed his words, she struggled to keep the tears at bay. All she had been thinking of was how happy she was to be married to Mark, and how exciting it was to be starting their life together. She had expected them to share everything, the good parts of life, the bad ones, and, yes, even meals. His response stunned sweet, innocent Beth.

It was a brief moment, but it knocked the wind out of her sails. The stage was set for their marriage. It was the moment that foretold of what was to come.

"No, this is mine," his words echoed in her head.

They ate the rest of their first meal together in silence.

After dinner, the tour resumed. He took her to a lookout point with a beautiful view of the river. The two stood there for over an hour, enjoying the gentle breeze coming across the river and the tranquil sounds of water rushing over the smooth rocks along the riverbed.

Evening had settled in and the air coming off the river was cool. Beth was getting chilled. She had seen romantic movies and knew what was about to happen. Mark was about to be a gentleman and slip his jacket over her shoulders.

She waited expectantly for several minutes. He didn't make a move.

"Maybe he needs a nudge," she thought.

"It's getting a little cool out here," she said.

No response.

Minutes ticked by and she remembered being told by an older woman that men aren't mind readers, so she decided to tell him what she needed. It wouldn't be nearly as chivalrous that way, but it would still feel romantic when he slipped his denim jacket around her.

"Mark, can I borrow your jacket? I'm getting pretty chilled with the breeze coming across the river."

His response was not what she had hoped for.

"No, you should have brought your own jacket."

It took her several seconds to soak in what he'd said.

"Are you serious?" she softly questioned. "I'm really cold."

"This is my jacket," he said. "It's not my fault you didn't bring your own. Maybe next time you'll think about that."

Day one of marriage and the romance Beth had felt in her heart only a few hours before was being doused by the cold waters of Mark's indifference.

Day one.

But Beth wasn't one to dwell on the negative.

"He's right, after all," she said to herself. "It's my own fault I didn't bring a jacket."

They headed to their cabin for the night. Day one was over, the foundation of their marriage had been laid.

As she lay in bed that night, his words echoed in her mind.

"This is mine," he had said.

The sandwich, the jacket… "No, this is mine."

Don't Pay the Bills

Once the honeymoon was over, the newlywed couple settled into a rented house in the tiny town where Beth grew up. Beth and Mark both worked at minimum wage jobs. They both worked full-time, but their income wasn't strong. It fell to Beth to take care of household finances. Each week was a struggle. Bills got paid first, gas was put in vehicles second, and groceries were purchased last.

In the second week of marriage, Mark started making purchases for himself. Hunting clothes, fishing gear, guns and ammo. In itself, there was nothing wrong with buying these things. Actually, these items are household staples for many families in the South. But there wasn't enough money in the household finances to pay for these things. Mark began spending his paychecks before he came home on paydays, and Beth was left to use every penny of her paychecks to pay bills and buy groceries.

She didn't want to be one of those wives who nagged, but she had to say something.

"Mark, we can't afford all this hunting stuff. You've got to stop spending money."

No response.

"Mark," she said again, "you have to quit spending money on extra stuff. I want you to be able to have all of these things, but we absolutely cannot afford to spend money like this."

Again, Mark didn't respond.

Week after week he continued to come home with more stuff. It reached the point where there was no money for food.

"Mark, after I pay the bills this week, there's no money left. We won't be able to buy groceries."

His response to their situation was, "So, don't pay the bills."

"Did he just tell me not to pay the bills?" she asked herself. "Did he seriously just tell me not to pay the bills??"

She had never even considered skipping the bills. It wasn't right. It was irresponsible. She couldn't do that.

With his frivolous spending and her determination to do the right thing, the bills got paid, but they had to live off ramen. Week after week of ramen.

But he had his stuff. The stuff he was buying for himself. All those unnecessary purchases. At least he could show his friends and family all the stuff he had accumulated, and tell them, "This is mine."

Yes, Master

The initial weeks of marriage passed slowly by. The two went to work every day, slept next to each other every night, had sex, and did the things most married people do. Beth did all the housekeeping and cooking, with the exception of the one time Mark told her she was mopping wrong. He grabbed the mop and showed her how to clean the floors by his standards. And so, thinking the way she was mopping was somehow inferior, she mopped the floor the way he wanted her to for a bit. But, at least for a brief moment, he was mopping the floor himself.

Beth tried very hard to be a good wife. She brought his meals to him while he sat in his favorite chair. She washed his clothes and cleaned his home. She did these things to show her love for him.

One day, after a long day of work, he demanded she take off his work boots for him because he was too tired to do it himself. She loved him deeply, so she did as he told her.

And he demanded she remove his boots for him every day for the next 25 years.

Once he got used to having her take off his boots and wait on him hand and foot, he ordered her to take his truck to the gas station and fill it up with fuel every time it needed gas.

"Why can't you do it on your way home from work? That's what I do with my vehicle," she said.

"I'm too tired. Just do it, Beth."

He got home from work, ate and watched TV, while she drove to the station to fuel up his truck. Again, she loved him deeply, so she did as he told her.

On top of filling up his truck with gas every few days, when his truck had a low tire, he ordered her to take it to the air pump at the gas station and fill the tire with air. She did as he told her.

Again.

After weeks of airing up his low tire for him, she asked, "Why don't you stop at the tire shop on your way home from work one day this week and get the tire fixed?"

"Just go air up my tire and stop asking questions."

So, she did. She did everything he asked. She thought she was being a good wife.

Sometimes it seemed to Beth as though there were shadows over their marriage, but in spite of this feeling, she loved Mark very much. He was the sunshine in her days. Her world revolved around him. She realized there were some negatives, but she was learning to overlook them. Life was happier that way.

She was hopelessly, ridiculously in love. It was sickening.

Kiss Me Not

Three months after their wedding day, Mark was sitting in the rocking chair in their sparsely furnished living room. Beth sat on the floor facing him, her arms resting on his knees. She looked at him adoringly. She wanted to kiss him so badly, to lavish her love on him. So, she raised up on her knees and leaned in to kiss his lips. She could hardly contain the love she had for him.

As her lips neared his, he turned his head away. She thought he was being playful, so she leaned in to try again. For a second time he dodged her kiss.

"What's wrong?" she asked.

"I don't like kissing," he flatly said.

Beth pulled back.

"Why?" she asked, entirely caught off-guard by his words.

"I just don't."

"You liked kissing when we were dating. What changed?" she asked while pushing back tears.

"I don't like it anymore," he said.

"I do like kisses..." she said softly, almost to herself.

But it didn't matter. He had taken his stand. No more kissing. In a matter of seconds, he had taken away a part of their relationship Beth loved. In an instant, everything changed.

Time passed. She tried to respect him and not ask for kisses, but she eventually started trying to kiss him again. He allowed it, but he didn't like it. Knowing he hated every kiss took the joy and passion out of those moments. But she still kissed him. She still tried to have a connection with him. It was hard to do. She was the only one trying.

Physical touch was important for Beth. It was the way she gave and felt love. He took away the joy of kissing, and then he took away something else she loved. He stopped holding her hand. When it started happening, she thought maybe it was a normal thing. She didn't know of many married couples who held hands, so maybe this was a natural distancing that happened between married people. But she didn't like it. They didn't have to stop holding hands just because they were married.

"I refuse to lose this part of our relationship too," she thought, so she continued trying to hold his hand. In the car, walking in the mall, sitting next to each other in lawn chairs at cookouts, wherever.

As she tried to keep this part of their relationship alive, his response to hand-holding changed. Rather than simply releasing her hand, as he'd been doing, he began to shake his hand free of her grasp. It was as though her touch repulsed him. He began to recoil when she reached out to take his hand. If she managed to grab his hand, he would violently shake free of the grip. He seemed disgusted.

She began to feel ugly. He didn't want to kiss her, didn't want to hold her hand, didn't even want to make sure she had grocery money to keep from starving.

Only a few months into the marriage, and thoughts of, "Am I not good enough for him? Is there something wrong with me?" flooded her mind.

As he sat in the living room watching TV on a beautiful Saturday morning, she told him, "I need you to tell me I'm pretty, even if you have to lie."

"Yeah, you're pretty," he said without ever taking his eyes off the screen.

"I need to hear it sometimes," she said.

He told her she was pretty a year later, too, when she told him again, "Mark, I need you to tell me I'm pretty, even if you have to lie." And so, he told her she was pretty. That was the only time he said it that year too.

Each year, when she got to feeling especially ugly, she would tell him the same thing and he would respond the same way. He never told her unless she asked him to.

So, once a year he told her she was pretty because she told him she needed to hear it.

Shut Your Mouth

As they were sitting at their favorite drive-in restaurant enjoying some burgers and fries, Mark turned the radio up loud.

"Can we turn it down a little?" Beth asked. "It's kind of loud."

"No, I can hear you chewing, and I can't stand it!"

"You're turning up the radio so you can't hear me eating?" she asked.

"Yes, it's driving me nuts!" he said.

"Well, I'm eating… I'm supposed to make chewing noises. What else am I supposed to do?"

"Chew with your mouth closed," he said.

"I AM chewing with my mouth closed," Beth replied.

"Well, you're too noisy so the radio is staying on."

From that moment on, anytime when Beth ate, Mark would turn on music or turn up the TV. He got angry if she ate chips or crunchy foods. Beth changed the way she ate because Mark's reaction to her chewing embarrassed her deeply. So, she tried to only eat soft foods around him, and she didn't fully chew her food. She would lightly chew it until it got soft enough to be swallowed. Sometimes she went to the bedroom to eat meals.

Even though she tried her best to chew silently, there were times when he could still hear the sounds of her eating, and he made sure to complain about it. To the point where she was always ashamed to eat when he or other people were around. At work, with family, she was always worried everyone was focusing on the sound of her chewing her food.

It became such an obsession for Mark that the need to keep quiet also became an obsession for Beth.

You're Not a Looker, Beth

Beth had a decent figure, long legs, and she was tall and slender. She had long brown hair and pretty blue eyes. She tanned easily and kept a nice bronze glow during the summer months. Overall, she didn't look bad. She wasn't the prettiest girl on the planet, but she wasn't the ugliest either.

Mark stared at her one Saturday morning.

"Why don't you do your hair blonde?" he suggested.

To which Beth replied, "Because my hair is brown."

"You would look hot as a blonde," he said.

"But," Beth responded, "my hair is brown. It's always been brown. This is the color my hair is."

"I'm just saying you would look sexy with blonde hair."

Maybe it was innocent, but it hurt. Did he think her brown hair wasn't attractive? Only blondes could be sexy? She tried not to let it bother her, but it stuck in her mind.

Over the years he told her repeatedly that he wanted her to have blonde hair.

She finally caved and bought a home hair kit. Boy, that was a mistake! She bleached her pretty brown hair, and when the process was finished, her hair was bright orange and fried to a crisp!

She had tried to give Mark what he wanted, and now she was laughable. She looked like a clown. A literal clown. She had destroyed her hair trying to look nice for him.

"Why didn't I leave my hair alone? I liked my brown hair," she thought as tears ran down her cheeks. "Why am I not pretty enough for him?"

It wasn't just that he occasionally suggested she go blonde, but he would compare her to other women.

"What would it take for you to look like her?" he'd ask.

"You should straighten your hair."

"You should get your hair done super curly like that girl's."

"You know that tall, lanky blonde that was at church Sunday? When I saw her, I almost drooled all over myself!" he told her.

He never once looked at Beth and told her she was beautiful just the way she was. He constantly asked her why she couldn't look like someone else.

And for 25 years, it wrecked the image she saw every time she looked in the mirror.

Bedroom Bond

Time passed. Beth and Mark moved to a couple of different locations. As is common with many young adults, their jobs changed periodically. When she was 23 years old, Beth was working two jobs and standing on her feet waiting on customers 70 hours a week. Mark worked one job with hours that fluctuated depending on the weather. They had a slightly stronger income than what they'd had in the beginning, but it wasn't enough to pay all the bills plus support his spending habits. Beth struggled. She did the best she could with what she had.

After a particularly difficult week, Beth asked Mark, "Can you work a little more? We really need more money."

"I can't, Beth. You have no idea how hard it is to do the work I do. I spend every day in the woods, pressing through underbrush and briars to repaint forest boundary lines. It's difficult."

"You get paid for the miles you cover while you're painting the boundary lines, right? Instead of doing only one mile a day, can you possibly do a mile-and-a-half or two miles?"

"Beth, you don't understand. I can't. It's not like taking a walk down the highway. I'm stooping to go under limbs, stepping over logs, and constantly fighting thick undergrowth. I know it's only $15 a mile, but I can't do more than that in a day," he responded.

"I get that it's hard, but you leave home at 7:00 in the morning and you're back home by noon. You're working 25 hours a week. I know you're working really hard, but my jobs aren't easy either. I'm on my feet 70 hours a week serving customers at the restaurant and checking out people's groceries at the store. I don't think I can handle working more hours, not while I'm taking care of the cooking, housework, and kids too. We really need your part of the income to be stronger. I know it's terrible of me to ask, but we are financially going under," she said.

"I can't do it, Beth. I'm not going to put in more hours."

There was nothing she could do, aside from continuing to rob Peter to pay Paul.

In spite of the financial struggles, during this part of their marriage, something delightful happened. The intensity of their sex life skyrocketed. They were enjoying each other's bodies almost every day of the week and exploring pleasure in ways they had never done before. It was an amazing time of intimacy and bonding. Their relationship outside the bedroom became stronger than ever too. Their bond became so incredibly strong that people outside the family commented on how well they got along and how beautifully they interacted with each other.

Beth often thought to herself, "It's because of all the steamy, yummy sex!"

Aside from money issues, Beth thought their marriage couldn't possibly get any better. It was incredible! The sex made it that way.

Three months into this beautiful season of their relationship, Mark took it all away.

He took away the sex that had created such an amazing bond between them. As she was trying to seduce him one night, he told her he couldn't keep having sex so often. So, they didn't share each other's bodies that night. Or very often after that. The sex that they were once having five times a week slowed down to twice a week. It was still nice, but the heat was gone. Beth found it hard to be passionate after her husband restricted their times of intimacy.

"I need his touch, his kisses, the warmth of his body," she thought to herself.

As time went on, he continued to take away the things that mattered to her, little by little. Within a few short years of their wedding day, that day when she had been so incredibly enthralled with the idea of being

his wife, her love had begun the slow,
painful process of dying.

Beth Needs a Hug

As the years slowly passed, and her love grew dim, Beth desired physical contact more than ever before. After years of being denied or mocked when she told Mark the things that she needed, she got brave enough to make another request of her husband.

"I really need you to hug me," she told him. "Like ten times a day. I need more than just the ordinary, cursory goodbye-I'm-leaving-for-work hug in the mornings. I really need lots of hugs from you. And to be honest, hugs while I'm working in the kitchen are my favorite."

He didn't say anything.

But she did notice he increased the number of hugs he was giving her. He went from zero up to a whopping one hug a day.

"It's like he's just giving me the tiniest bit of effort, so I'll leave him alone. Kind of like tossing a dog a bone to get it to quit barking," she thought.

To Pee or Not to Pee

After a year of painting boundary lines, Mark quit his job and got involved in factory work. His workplace was an hour from home and put a lot of miles on his truck.

"I need to put my truck in the shop to get some work done on it," he told Beth. "I'll need you to wake up early in the mornings and take me to work, and then come pick me up after work in the afternoons until I get my truck back."

That was fine with Beth. She didn't mind helping him with that. She definitely wanted him to be able to go to work.

So, she woke up at 2:00 in the mornings and made the trips to Mark's workplace while his truck was being repaired.

After a few days, Mark got the call that his truck was ready to be picked up.

He called Beth, "I need you to get to my job an hour early today so you can park close to the gate, and I can beat the crowd at clock-out time. Then we'll hurry to pick up my truck from the shop before they close."

Beth did as he asked and arrived an hour early to get a good parking spot close to the entrance of the factory. It had taken her an hour to drive to his job, and after an hour of being parked, she really needed a potty break.

"Is there a way I can use the bathroom in your factory?" she texted him.

"No, they won't allow outsiders to come in."

"I'll be back in a minute. I need to find a gas station so I can go pee," she texted.

"No! You stay right where you are or you'll lose your parking spot. I'll be out in a minute."

She kept her car parked and waited for him, but she really needed a restroom.

He clocked out, hurried to the parking lot, and hopped in the driver's seat. They left quickly. They had a limited amount of time to get to the mechanic's shop before it closed.

"Mark, I need to stop for a restroom as soon as we get a chance," she told him.

"We don't have time. We have to get there before the shop closes, and it's a two-hour drive. There's no way we're stopping."

Beth loosened her seatbelt so it wouldn't press on her bladder. She understood the urgency of getting to the shop before it closed down for the day. But she was also feeling another kind of urgency that was impossible to ignore.

After an hour on the road, she was in pain and began to cry.

"Mark, I can't help it. We're going to have to find a bathroom. I'm hurting so bad."

He kept driving.

"If I don't feel the need to pee, then you don't feel the need to pee either," he angrily told her.

They finally made it to the auto shop. She made a beeline for the restroom while Mark paid the cashier.

Over the years, he echoed his words again and again.

If he, Beth and the kids were traveling, he would tell them, "If I don't need the restroom, nobody else needs it either."

Or he would say, "If I'm not hungry, that means nobody else is hungry either."

Or, "If I don't have a headache, then nobody else does either."

He meant every word.

Bringing Down the House

During the first few years of married life, two sons and a daughter had been born to the couple. Beth had enrolled one of the kids in a pre-school program in a neighboring town. Day one was a meet and greet. She was one of many moms present in the large crowd. As her eyes skimmed over all the parents in the room, one of the faces caught her attention. It was her classmate from high school. When the program ended, Beth and her old classmate talked with each other and exchanged phone numbers.

She was absolutely thrilled to have run into her friend. When the weekend came, she gave her a call. As the conversation began, Mark started being noisy. It was normal behavior for him. Anytime she was on the phone he would deliberately make excessive noise. The longer she stayed on the phone, the louder he would get. Crumpling potato chip bags, talking to her while she was trying to have a conversation with the other person, turning up the volume on the TV. It's just what he did.

The phone call with her friend began the same way. Mark saw she was on the phone, so he started being loud. He was a lazy man and seldom got out of his recliner if he didn't have to, so Beth left the noise of the living room and walked into the bedroom. Because he seldom got up, she was highly surprised when he got out of his chair and followed her. He was steadily talking loudly, and Beth was having a hard time carrying on the phone conversation. She kept trying to walk away from him, but he followed her relentlessly. She finally stepped into the master bathroom and locked the door behind her.

"Now, it's quiet," she thought to herself.

She sat on the lid of the toilet while she and her friend chatted. It was nice.

For about 30 seconds.

Mark tried to open the door and realized it was locked. He began banging loudly on the bathroom door. His fists pounded the door so violently, the walls of the room were shaking.

Beth's friend heard the commotion.

"Are you ok?" she asked.

Embarrassed, Beth said, "Ummm... yeah, I'm fine. There's just somebody at the door..."

Mark began to use more force in an effort to break down the door.

As the pounding became louder, her friend asked again, "Are you sure you're ok?"

"I need to go," Beth told her friend.

She ended the call and opened the door so he wouldn't break it. She knew if the door got broken, she'd be the person who had to find the money to buy a new one, and she'd be the person who had to install it. Opening the door to stop Mark from destroying it was the best avenue to take.

She began to open the door, and he grabbed it and pulled it away from her. As she stood in the frame of the bathroom doorway, she looked at him. He had such anger in his eyes. She didn't understand. She never understood why he did the things he did.

She never talked with her friend again.

Things Get Physical

For their 10-year anniversary, Beth planned a big party complete with live music by a local band. Family and friends were invited to have punch, cake, and enjoy the music in celebration of ten years of marriage. Beth flitted about from one area of the party to another, wearing her wedding veil from that fateful day 10 years prior, when she was clad in her floor-length wedding dress and walking the aisle with her life flashing before her eyes. Today she was having a great time.

When it was time for refreshments to be served, Mark and Beth cut the cake. They'd had it specially made to match their original wedding cake. It was two-tiered and iced with white and blue icing.

As the two prepared to take a bite of their cake, Beth was tempted to dot Mark's nose with cake icing. She didn't do it on their wedding day because he had smiled and told her if she did it, she would regret it. So, she played it safe. But this day was a different story. She was feeling super happy and playful, so she decided to carefully boop his nose with a piece of cake. She left the tiniest dot of icing on his nose. It was a cute moment.

But the cute part didn't last long.

Mark rammed his piece of cake into Beth's face. He began smearing it all over her face and into her hair. He pressed aggressively against her face until she wasn't able to stand up anymore. Once she fell onto the floor, he sat straddle of her and continued grinding cake and icing into her face. Beth struggled. She couldn't get away. He had her pinned. So, she stopped struggling. In her mind, sometimes aggressive animals would leave their prey alone once the prey ceased to struggle. So, she lay still and allowed Mark to continue his attack.

Once he was finished, he stood up and walked away laughing. It wasn't a happy laugh. It was more of a maniacal chuckle.

"I told you not to do it," he said as he walked away from his incapacitated wife. "I told you not to do it and you did it anyway. I bet you won't do it again. I bet you learned your lesson," he said as he chuckled.

Beth shakily got up from the floor. She made her way to the kitchen sink and began to wash her face. She tried to laugh it off. She didn't want the guests to know it upset her. But her guests weren't stupid. Once she cleaned up, she glanced around, and the party guests were looking at her with pity in their eyes. The party that had been fun and lively a few minutes before, had now completely died. No one wanted to be there anymore.

Road Trip

It rarely happened, but every now and then Beth woke up with a travel bug. She absolutely had to go somewhere on a road trip, even if it was only for a day.

One Sunday morning, she woke up and wanted to go to one of Arkansas's lovely state parks. The one she had in mind was a park she and her family had never visited before.

She convinced Mark, and they and the kids loaded up for a day trip. She punched the name of the park into her phone's GPS, and away they went with Beth behind the wheel.

After two long hours of driving, they arrived at a different state park, one they'd never heard of. The GPS had taken them to the wrong place. Mark had been pleasant during the trip, but once they arrived at the wrong destination, he became very angry.

"I've never heard of this park," Beth said. "Let's stop and check out the hiking trails."

"Stay in the truck! Find the park we're supposed to be going to!" he ordered.

Beth punched the name of the park into her GPS again, and it loaded a new set of directions. She continued to drive as Mark sat in the passenger seat complaining.

"Can't you drive faster?" he asked. "I'm sick of riding!"

"Stop hitting all the bumps in the road! You deliberately find every single bump and pothole in the road and run right through them, don't you? You need to drive like you know what you're doing!" he said.

By the time they arrived at the correct location an hour later, Mark was raging. There was no reason Beth could see for his anger, but he was incredibly mad. He had berated her incessantly.

She parked the truck, and the kids all clambered out. Beth saw that there was a boardwalk that wound through the swamp, so she pointed it out to the kids, and they headed toward it. Mark did too.

Her heart was aching, and she was silently crying. She hurried to lead the pack so everyone would be behind her, and no one could see her tears. It seemed like she was always finding ways to hide the tears.

After they had thoroughly explored the area, Beth's silent tears had dried and she wanted her picture taken by the large, wooden state park sign. She handed her camera to one of the kids, and she went over to pose by the sign. Mark didn't like having his picture taken, but when he saw Beth posing to have her picture made, he hurried to stand beside her. She wanted to tell him to go away, to get out of her picture because he was ruining it. But she didn't. That would be mean, and she wasn't a mean person. So, she allowed him to stand beside her. She fixed a convincing smile on her face and had her picture taken with Mark by her side.

Beth Fights an Intruder

There was a middle-aged woman in the tiny town where Mark and Beth lived. Her name was Mary. She had grown up in that town, went to school at the local school, went to church at the local church, and she'd recently married a local man who later had to divorce her because she had a drug addiction.

The drug addiction caused her to lose everything. Her children had abandoned her. She'd sold her home. She'd wrapped her car around a tree while driving under the influence. And she was jobless – by choice.

All the people of the town had a soft spot in their hearts for her. As she roamed the streets homelessly, everyone tried to help her. They'd take her in for a few days until her behavior became too much. They'd give her clothes and food. They'd drive her places if she needed to go somewhere. They'd even offer to help her get jobs or take her to a rehab program.

In spite of all the help her friends and neighbors offered, she chose the drugs. She chose homelessness.

Beth sat on her front porch one Sunday morning, enjoying the breeze. She saw Mary walking along the road headed in her direction. Beth wanted to go inside her house and hide, but Mary had already seen her sitting outside. Beth had dealings with Mary in the past. She had let her live in her house, and sleep on her sofa, for nine days. She'd helped her get an apartment and a job. But Mary didn't want to go to work, so Beth had made her leave. She told Mary she wasn't going to help her if she wasn't willing to help herself.

As Mary neared the house on this morning, Beth noticed she had electrodes showing near the collar of her shirt, the kind hospitals use when they're checking a patient's heart. Beth didn't ask. She didn't want to know.

Mary seemed… off. Like she was high. She spoke to Beth, but nothing made sense.

"Let me go call someone to give you a ride, Mary," Beth said as she stood up and went into her house. She needed to get Mary to leave, and getting a ride for her was the only way she could think of to do that. The ride Beth had in mind was in a deputy's car, and the destination would be a women's shelter.

As she started to shut the door behind her, she realized Mary had followed her into her living room. Beth had expected her to wait patiently on the porch like a good guest, but she didn't.

"Mary, wait right here. I've got to go to the bedroom and get my phone. I'll be right back."

Beth wanted to sneak away to use the phone so she could privately call the police to come pick up Mary and take her to a shelter. That was her plan.

She walked down the hallway to the bedroom where Mark was. He was standing beside his nightstand where he kept his home defense pistol. He was scrolling through his phone when Beth came into the room. He was standing six feet from her but never looked up.

As she stepped inside the room and reached to close the door behind her, she felt resistance. The door wouldn't close.

She turned around to see Mary standing in the doorway blocking the door.

"Mary, you can't be in here," Beth said. "You have to leave."

"Why?" Mary asked with a glazed look in her eyes.

"Because this is my bedroom," Beth said, "and you can't be in here."

"Why?" Mary repeated.

Beth shouted, "This is my bedroom, and you're not allowed to be in here! Get out! Just get out of my house!"

Mark never once looked up from his phone.

He had a homeless drug addict who had forced her way into his bedroom, a wife who was screaming louder than she'd ever screamed in her life, and he never even noticed.

Beth continued screaming at Mary. She started shoving her out of the room. But people who are high on meth are invincible. They're much stronger than they should be. As was the case with Mary. She was a skinny woman, just a wisp of a thing, yet Beth could hardly get her to budge.

As Beth struggled to get Mary out of the room, she shouted, "Mark, get your gun!"

He didn't respond.

"Mark! Put your phone down and get your pistol!" she shouted again.

He finally snapped out of whatever world he was in. He grabbed his pistol and followed Beth as she tried to wrangle Mary. Beth never stopped screaming at her. It didn't even sound like her own voice. Beth had lost control of herself. She screamed until she felt like her throat was bleeding. And she shoved and shoved, making progress with relocating Mary a couple of inches at a time.

Mary wasn't fighting Beth; she was simply resisting. And she was like a fortress.

She didn't want Mary to die. She didn't want her to be shot, but if Mary started to fight Beth, she knew Mark would have to shoot, and he'd be justified in doing so.

After several minutes of struggling, Beth was finally able to shove Mary out of the front door of their home. And then she shoved her off the porch and out into the yard. She was exhausted, but she was glad Mark didn't have to shoot.

As Mark held his aim on Mary, Beth stepped aside and called the sheriff's office. A deputy came out within minutes, but Mary had already wandered off by the time he got there.

"Yeah," the deputy said, "we've had several run-ins with her today. She keeps getting in cars with people, forcing her way into people's houses. We were about to arrest her earlier, but she said she was having chest pains, so we took her to the hospital instead. Apparently, she didn't stay very long. She's on meth. She won't be in her right mind for a while. Nothing we can do since she's already gone but give us a call if she comes back."

Beth was shaken. Her stomach felt like it had a boulder in it. She'd never had to manhandle anyone like that. And she never wanted to again.

For days, her mind kept replaying the events. How could Mark stand there so nonchalantly while there was an intruder in their bedroom? Why didn't Mark shove Mary out of the house? He's bigger and stronger, so why did he leave it to Beth? Maybe in his mind it was a girl fight so he shouldn't intrude?

It didn't make sense.

Once she'd calmed down, Beth's heart began to ache for Mary.

"One day," she told Mark, "someone is going to find Mary dead in a ditch."

And five years later, someone did.

The Devil is Coming

The kids were young, and Beth was itching for a long weekend trip. They had the bare minimum of cash, but she wanted to make a dash to the Arkansas-Missouri line.

They went on a simple camping trip next to a beautiful Missouri lake. Geese walked up to their campsite several times a day hoping for handouts. The kids were having a lot of fun. It was also Fourth of July weekend, so the little family got to see lots of fireworks being displayed over the lake.

After a couple of days of camping, it was time to make the trip home. They had a little cash leftover, so they decided to buy tickets for a cave tour along their southward travel route.

The cavern wasn't anything spectacular, but there was a small room in the cave that was illuminated with red lights. The glow made the small room look fiery.

As they stood there amidst a small group of other tourists, Mark held their youngest child, who was two years old.

As the tour guide spoke, the red lights started flashing.

"Look!" Mark loudly told his son. "The devil is coming to get you! See that red light? The devil is coming to get you!"

Their son screamed and cried and tried to get away, but Mark held him tight.

"He's coming to get you! He's going to take you away! The devil is coming to get you!"

"Mark," Beth said in a hushed voice, "stop that! People are staring at you!"

But he didn't stop. He kept on tormenting their child.

Beth reached over and pulled their son away from Mark. She held him and consoled him. She told him the devil wasn't coming to get him, that his daddy was just being silly.

But sometimes the damage can't be reversed. And sometimes there are nightmares. And sometimes the nightmares last for years.

Mark Ditches Construction

Time marched on. Money was tight. Money was always tight. She regularly told her husband there wasn't enough money for one purchase or another. His response was, "I'm buying it anyway. I can always make more money."

So, his spending continued, and so did Beth's struggle to make ends meet. One day he proposed a financial plan that would make it easier for him to make purchases. He explained how a man shouldn't work only to pay bills, but he should have money in his pocket as well. He said he decided to start giving her $500 a week to pay the bills and buy the groceries, and he would keep any part of his paycheck over that amount.

Beth agreed. She did the best she could with that allowance, but it wasn't enough. With a $600 mortgage, a $500 truck payment, car insurance, the phone bill, lights, water, gas and food, that allowance just wasn't enough to stretch.

Sometimes she had a job, sometimes she didn't. She was raising a houseful of babies, doing all the cleaning, cooking and lawn maintenance, so it was difficult for her to leave home to work. Eventually the bills got out of control and their mobile home was repossessed.

They moved in with Beth's mom and began the process of building themselves a house a little at a time. Construction moved along swiftly during the first few months. Beth and Mark worked as a team, building the house themselves. They had the frame up and rafters. The house wasn't in the dry yet. They still needed to put plywood on the roof and walls. But construction was moving along quickly and smoothly.

And one day Mark just quit.

He stopped building. He didn't say why. He simply stopped working and sat in his mother-in-law's house watching TV every day after work and all weekend long.

Beth had no interest in continuing to live in her mother's house. She was married with three kids. It was juvenile to keep living in her mom's house when they could build their own.

So, Beth gritted her teeth and tried to finish building the house by herself. She worked hard. She never minded working. But this job was too big for her. She kept bending the nails and missing the studs as she used one arm to hold the plywood against the wall frame and her other arm to hammer the nails.

She gave it her all… but she couldn't do it alone. After weeks of struggling yet gaining no ground, she had no choice but to walk away from the project.

They had been married 15 years at that point. She had been struggling for those 15 years.

She had held disappointment and pain in her heart for 15 years. She had kept a false smile on her face for 15 years.

Depression kicked in and thoughts of suicide began to take over. It's not something she wanted. She had always wanted to live. Life was something precious and to be valued, and Beth was always looking for the positives in every situation. But something within her broke when Mark left her to build the house alone. And, after 15 years of smiling through the heartache, her defenses dropped, and she began to court the demons in her soul.

It was a battle she couldn't tell anyone about. She loved her children more than life itself. She would never want to leave them. Ever. But she began to feel a dark presence over her, like a cloud that hung just above her head everywhere she went. She fought to resist ending her life. It was a silent battle she fought alone.

The battle lasted several months. In the end, she won. But she had scars on her soul to remind her of how hard she'd had to fight just to stay alive.

Mark's Shopping Spree

After several months of Mark watching TV in his mother-in-law's house and not working on his own home construction, he found a house they could buy in another town.

"Finally!" Beth thought.

It's not what she wanted. She wanted a house they had built together and didn't owe a mortgage on, but Beth was quite happy about it anyway. Of course, she tried to be happy about life in general. She always tried to look at the positive side of every situation. He never said it, but she knew Mark hated that facet of her personality.

They moved to the new house. It was modest, but nice. The real estate agent gave them a gift card to use at a local retail store. So, they went shopping to get some essentials for the house. The card was an especially nice gift because they had spent their last dime on closing costs of the home purchase. Beth and Mark were beyond broke.

Her plan was to buy essentials like toilet paper, dish soap, a mop, broom, and other cleaning supplies. But Mark began loading the shopping cart with expensive towels, bathroom rugs, and other fancy bathroom accessories. Beth told him he was spending all the gift card money, but he kept adding more expensive items to the cart. The gift card had $700 on it to begin with. After they checked out of the store, there was only $30 left. They hadn't bought any of the household essentials on Beth's list. All they had purchased were the costly bathroom decor items Mark had tossed in the shopping cart.

Beth's heart sank when she realized Mark had spent all the money. They were moving into a house that someone else had previously lived in. Everything needed to be cleaned and sanitized. Toilets and bathtubs needed to be bleached, floors needed to be mopped, carpeting needed to be shampooed. They had none of the supplies they needed to clean their new house.

In 15 years of marriage, Mark had never apologized to her, but as they walked across the parking lot to their car, he said, "I'm sorry."

"It'll be ok," Beth said.

Push-Mowing Her Life Away

After the newness of moving in wore off, the little family got into a normal routine. Beth and Mark both worked full-time. He came home after work, sat in his recliner and watched TV. He spent the weekends the same way – sitting in his chair and watching TV for 48 hours straight, with the exceptions of bedtime and bathroom breaks.

Beth spent the hours after work cooking and cleaning and caring for the kids. Her weekends were spent cleaning the house, washing laundry, and doing lawn maintenance.

She occasionally asked for help with household tasks like unloading the dishwasher or trimming the hedges, but Mark's response was to continue sitting in his chair and watching TV. Beth was left to tackle all of the responsibilities herself.

Both of them worked more than 40 hours a week. Their workdays were long. Household chores required a lot of time, especially mowing the yard. They didn't have a riding mower, so Beth used a push mower. She spent five hours each weekend of the warm-weather season mowing the yard. In south Arkansas, where they lived, grass grew for about six months of the year. The time it consumed, and the heat of the sun, began to be a burden for Beth.

"Mark, will you please start helping me with yard work? It's just too much for me to do all by myself. If I was a housewife, it wouldn't be a problem. I could just add it to the list of chores I'd be doing throughout the day. But I'm working full-time, and I just can't do it all by myself."

"No. I'm allergic to grass," he replied with a touch of aggravation in his voice.

"I'm allergic to grass too. Just take an allergy pill and wear a dust mask," she said.

"No, I'm not working in the yard."

"Will you at least pick up sticks before I mow?" she pleaded.

"No," he wagged his head in frustration. "I'm not doing yard work!"

So, Beth came up with another idea.

"Will you pay someone to come out and cut the grass every other week? You could pay for it out of your pocket money. I've already talked with a gardener. It's not going to cost much," she said.

Mark glared at her like that was the stupidest thing he'd ever heard.

"No, I'm not spending money on that," he said as he turned his gaze back to the TV without batting an eye.

That was the end of the conversation. The yard work was left for Beth to bear.

It wasn't as though Mark couldn't afford it. As per the rule set several years before, he put $500 a week into the household finances, and he kept the rest of his paycheck for himself. Over the years, jobs had changed, and his career had advanced. He was earning a larger paycheck than he did in the early years of their marriage. Each week, $500 went into the budget for Beth to use for bills and groceries, and $600 went into Mark's pocket. And he spent every dime of that fun money on himself - $30,000 a year. But he wasn't willing to spend $200 a month to hire someone to keep the lawn managed.

He simply didn't care.

"Maybe if I stop cutting the grass and let the lawn get shaggy…" Beth thought. "Maybe, just maybe, that will spur him into helping me."

It was a manipulative plan, and she knew it, but she was desperate for help. Over the weeks, the grass in their yard grew so tall that when Beth walked across the lawn, the grass was brushing her thighs. It was a terrible mess. Even the neighbors had started talking about it. Some of them offered to come over and cut the grass for them. It embarrassed Beth, but it didn't faze Mark at all.

"Mark, our neighbor from a few miles up the road saw me outside and stopped to tell me he'd be happy to haul his riding mower to our house and cut the grass for us."

"Tell him to come on over and cut it if he wants to," he told her, and went right back to watching TV.

Her plan didn't work. Mark didn't care. He didn't care at all.

But Beth did, so she got the mower out and went to work.

Again.

Alone.

Lone Wolf

"I think I'm going to buy a motorcycle," he told her.

"We can't afford a motorcycle," she said.

"No, listen to my idea," Mark responded. "I can fill up the motorcycle with $20 of gas each week and ride to work all week on that single tank of gas. With fuel prices being so high right now, this will save us tons of money," he said.

"But we'd have a monthly bike payment plus the cost of insurance. And what about when the weather is rainy or it's below freezing outside? You won't be able to ride the motorcycle to work in those weather conditions," she said.

"They make special clothing that will keep me warm and dry when the weather is bad. I can drive the bike every day," he told her.

"How will we pay for it?" Beth asked.

"I'll pay for it out of my pocket money," he said. "And the brand of motorcycle I'm going to buy has a great resale value. If I decide to sell it, I can basically get the same price I paid for it new. There's no way to lose!"

She didn't like the plan at all, but she reluctantly agreed to it. The idea of saving gas money appealed to her, and if he was going to pay for the motorcycle himself out of his play money, it should work out really well.

So, Mark got his motorcycle license and bought the bike. He rode it to work every day.

When the first monthly statement came in the mail, she handed it to Mark.

"What's this?" he asked.

"It's your bike statement. It's time to make your first payment," she replied.

"I don't have the money this week. I need you to pay it," he said.

"You told me you'd be paying for it out of your fun money," she said.

"Yeah, but it costs too much. Just pay it out of the regular household budget."

"That's not at all what we agreed on, Mark."

But he refused to pay the bill, so Beth took care of it. And she did the same the next month, and the month after that, for years.

After he'd had the motorcycle a couple of months, he stopped driving it to work every day. He drove it once or twice a week and drove his truck on the other days.

"How come you're not taking your bike to work every day?" she asked.

"Some days it looks like it might rain, and I don't want to be out in it," he said.

"When you told me you wanted to buy a motorcycle, you said you'd buy special clothes so you could ride it in all kinds of weather," she responded.

"Yeah, but the highway gets slick when it rains, and I don't want to have a wreck."

Somehow it didn't surprise her that he had gone back on his word.

As the months progressed, and the random rain showers of summer were over, Mark still seldom rode his motorcycle.

"It's not rainy weather anymore," Beth said as winter approached. "Will you be riding your bike to work this week?"

"It's too danged cold to ride a motorcycle," he said.

"Why don't you buy some of those heated outfits they make for people who ride motorcycles?" she asked.

"Nah, that wouldn't be warm enough," he replied. "My hands would still get cold."

He had talked her into agreeing a motorcycle was a great way to save gas money. But in the end, she was paying the bike payments out of the household finances each month, she was paying the insurance each month, and she was having to scrape up enough money each week to put $100 worth of gas in Mark's pickup truck so he could drive to work.

Then one day a brilliant idea struck Beth. She figured out a way she could get a little enjoyment out of the motorcycle that was collecting dust in the carport.

"Hey, Mark, I have a great idea! I'd like you to start taking me for rides on your motorcycle," she told him. "That would be a lot of fun!"

"No, driving with a passenger can be dangerous," he said. "If you move at all, it could make me wreck the bike."

"I'll be perfectly still, I promise," she told him.

"Nah…" he said as he smiled, "I don't want to put a passenger seat on it. I like the lone wolf look."

"The lone wolf look… so, that's why he got the motorcycle… he thinks it makes him sexy…" she thought. "He doesn't want to look like he has a woman."

Beth was angry. But she didn't say a word. She held it inside, with so many of the other negatives in their relationship.

She never got to enjoy the motorcycle. He never put a passenger seat on it. She never rode it. And, one day after it had been sitting in the carport for a few years, Mark decided to sell it.

He sold it for $7,000. Half of the $14,000 he had paid for it... or rather, the $14,000 Beth had paid for it.

Playing Pool at the Bar

"Mark, can you call and let me know when you're going to be late coming home from work? I worry about you when you don't show up on time."

He didn't say anything.

She made this request of him many times over the course of the marriage. But to no avail.

He continued to periodically arrive home past his normal time without calling to let her know he was working late. On days when he was late getting home, she worried that he might have been in a wreck. Some days he was so late getting home that she called local hospitals to see if he had been admitted. And later on, he would pull up in the drive, perfectly fine. He had just worked late and didn't tell her.

One evening, he came home two hours late. Beth had been worried sick.

"Why are you so late?" she asked.

"I went to the bar with some of the guys after work to watch them play pool," he nonchalantly replied.

"You what? I was worried!" she said. "I was afraid something awful had happened to you! I even called the hospitals to see if you had been admitted to the emergency room!"

"Nah," he said, "I was just at the bar with the guys." Then he laughed. "There was this one slutty girl there who was sitting on the corner of the pool table telling us we could put a ball in her pocket anytime. She had her legs sprawled out along the edges of the table and wouldn't stop talking dirty."

Beth was stunned. Whenever he had been late getting home before, it was because he was working late, or he had been engrossed in conversation with someone after he clocked out. But this time he went to a bar? And entertained conversation with a woman who was talking dirty to him and the other guys?

She had no response. She couldn't find the words.

She never asked him to tell her when he was running late again. She wasn't sure she cared anymore.

Chimichanga

"Let's make a road trip," Mark said as he got out of bed Sunday morning.

Beth and the kids got dressed and everyone piled into the truck.

"Where are we going?" Beth asked.

"Oklahoma," he said.

"Don't you need to be at work this evening? Do we have time to drive that far?" she asked.

"There's a state park I want to check out. We won't stay long. I'll have time to get to work later," he assured her.

Mark drove all the way there. It was a beautiful day, and Beth was glad she was in the passenger seat so she could enjoy the scenery.

Occasionally, they would pass chicken farms, which are notoriously smelly places. When the scent of chicken manure would enter the cab of the truck, Mark would reach over and press Beth's knees together. He liked to shame her by insinuating that anything smelly must be coming from between her legs. It humiliated her and made her angry.

"Mark, stop," she told him.

But he didn't. He liked humiliating her that way.

A few chicken farms later, and they were pulling into the state park. It was a nice place, but they didn't stay long.

When they got in the truck to leave, Mark got in the driver's seat again.

"I need you to use the GPS on your phone and navigate us home," he told her.

"Ok," she said.

So, she punched in their home address and gave him directions as the GPS gave her updates.

Mark sped so he could make it to work on time. Everyone held on tight as their truck wound along the curvy road at a very fast pace. When they got into the city of Texarkana, she told him, "Take this exit."

"That can't be right," he said.

Beth checked the GPS again.

"Yeah, it says to take this exit," she said.

"Beth, that's not right! There's no way that's the exit we're supposed to take!" he shouted.

He pulled the truck into a parking area.

"Check the GPS again and find the right road!" he shouted.

Beth checked but nothing changed. It still showed the same exit. She even pulled out a paper map and it showed the same thing.

"Beth, if you can't do any better than that, you can get in the back seat with the kids!" he yelled.

He wasn't hitting her. He never hit her. But with each foul word, she felt as though he was knocking the wind from her lungs.

Beth wanted to open her door and get out of the truck. She wanted to walk the hundred miles back home. She couldn't stomach being in the truck with Mark anymore. She was so tired of him yelling at her and making her feel stupid. But she couldn't get out of the truck. Her kids were still in the back seat. They would go into a panic if she got out of the truck, so she stayed. She stayed for the kids.

Mark pulled up the GPS on his phone to check the directions.

"Oh, you're right," he said.

She had been telling him the right exit the whole time.

Did he apologize? No. He just started driving.

Mark was weird when it came to driving. He always wanted someone else in the truck to tell him if it was ok to merge into the neighboring lane. Beth was never allowed to take a nap in the passenger seat, because he demanded that she be constantly alert as to whether or not he could shift over into the left lane or the right lane on the interstate.

After him yelling at her and telling her to get in the back seat, she decided she wasn't going to tell him if it was safe to merge or not. All of the other drivers in the world use their mirrors. As far as she was concerned at this point in the trip, he could use the mirrors too. She couldn't care less if he wanted her to tell him when he could merge.

And that made him incredibly angry.

"Beth, can I get over?" he asked.

"I'm not sure. You should check your mirrors and see," she said.

"Beth! Can I get over or not?!"

"Maybe. Look and see if you can," she told him.

After a few miles, he pulled over on the shoulder of the freeway.

"If you're not going to help me drive, you can get over here and do it!" he yelled.

Beth got in the driver's seat. She dreaded driving when he was in the truck. He always berated her and told her how poorly she was driving. Every time she drove, he scolded her and told her she was a bad driver. He would go into a panic if they passed an exit they needed to take. He would yell, wag his head back and forth, throw his hands in the air, and try to make her feel stupid for missing it.

"You missed the exit!" he'd shout. "You missed the danged exit! Now what?! I can't believe you missed it!"

She would respond by calmly telling him, "All roads lead to our destination. All we have to do is find a different road or turn around and go back. It's nothing to panic about."

But he always went into a verbal frenzy if he thought they missed their turn.

Over the years, his words and his attitude had worn Beth down. She decided she needed to come up with her own personal word or phrase to keep herself calm when he went into a rage about her driving or navigation skills.

"What word can I use as my own personal calming tool?" she wondered. "What word… CHIMICHANGA!"

That was the word. Chimichanga. She had no idea why that's the word that came to mind, but it's what she chose.

Whenever Mark would yell at her because of her driving, she would quietly say the word chimichanga and it would make her smile. It relieved the tension of the moment, because she had a secret he knew nothing about. She had the word chimichanga.

The first time she used her coping word was on a road trip into north Arkansas. Mark wanted to check out a hiking trail in a mountainous area. They took both of their vehicles, so they could park at each end of the trail. One truck at the exit so they could ride back to the other truck they had parked at the trail entrance.

But there was a problem. They couldn't find the trail once they got to the mountain.

Mark was driving in front with Beth following behind. After much searching, evening was coming on and they still had not been able to find the trail. They had been driving the dusty gravel roads of the mountain for hours.

As dusk approached, Mark began speeding along the road. He was desperate to find the trail before dark.

Beth tried to keep up with him, but he was driving entirely too fast. As his truck drifted around curves and sprayed gravel everywhere, she prayed he wouldn't wrap his truck around a tree. Their youngest son was in the vehicle with him.

She had to back off. He was driving at extremely dangerous speeds on loose gravel, and she couldn't keep up. So, she let herself fall back quite a bit.

When his dust settled, she saw he had parked his truck in the middle of the road. She slowly pulled up behind him and stopped. He got out and came stomping toward her truck. She rolled down the window and he yelled at her.

"You need to keep up!" he shouted.

"Mark, you're driving way too fast. It's dangerous. You're going to end up sliding off the road. I can't keep up," she said.

"You're going to keep your butt up with me! Speed up!" he shouted.

"Chimichanga," she muttered under her breath as he stormed away.

And she smiled.

She was pleasantly surprised by how much control she felt after muttering a stupid little word.

It became a powerful coping mechanism over the course of their marriage. It helped keep her sane.

Chimichanga.

The Truth Came Out of the Closet

Mark was at work. Beth was at home doing household tasks. It was time to hang up laundry, so she was standing in front of her closet. Staring into it. Just standing there staring.

"I shouldn't be married to Mark. I should leave."

She delved deeply into thought as she stared at her clothing neatly hanging from the closet rod.

"But if I leave him, how will I pay for a house? How will I be able to provide for the kids?"

She continued to ponder as she stared blankly ahead.

"If I leave him and take the kids, they will still have to visit him on weekends, and I won't be there to protect them."

And that's when she knew she had to stay.

Her heart sank as she realized, "I'll never be loved. I'll never experience romance. I will live a life without passion. I just have to accept it. The kids are too important."

So, she stayed.

Ride or Die to Memphis

Mark wanted to take the kids to the zoo in Memphis. He told Beth about a week in advance so she could take a day off work. Taking the kids to the zoo sounded like a lot of fun. And she could use a day off work anyway, so why not?

The morning they left for the zoo, it was raining heavily. Many cars traveling the freeway had hydroplaned and hit the ditch. Beth had never seen so many cars that had wrecked at one time. For miles and miles, there were wrecked cars in the median and ditches of the interstate.

The rain was coming down hard.

As Mark drove, the truck began to accelerate. She quickly turned her head to look at the dash panel and check their speed.

70… 80… 90 miles an hour over asphalt that was flooded with rain water!

"Mark! Slow down!" Beth pleaded.

"You just have to know how to drive in this stuff," he said.

"Mark, look at all the cars in the ditch! We have to slow down!" she begged.

"Please... those people just don't know how to drive in the rain," he said as he laughed.

Beth prayed. And then prayed some more.

She didn't ask him to slow down again. She didn't want the children to hear her repeatedly pleading with him. She was afraid it would send them into a panic. So, she bit her tongue as he sped across the flooded roadway amidst the many other drivers who were sitting inside their wrecked cars.

Rain pelted the windshield and blurred her view out of the passenger window. She could still see wrecked cars as they flew past, but they seemed to be nothing more than shapeless blobs. Beth didn't feel like she could breathe. Every time the truck bogged down in water puddles, every time she felt the truck try to hydroplane or a sheet of water splash across the windshield, her body became stiff as a board in the expectation of hitting the ditch. After an hour of adrenaline and fear, she felt a wave of relief as they pulled into the parking lot of the zoo. Beth got the kids out of the truck just as the rain cleared away. She silently thanked God that they'd made it alive.

Ready, Aim...

Mark liked hunting and fishing. He watched videos and TV shows about such things, and he was always researching the best gear to buy. He especially liked guns. When it was all said and done, over the total course of their marriage, he had accumulated around 30 guns of different types. About 10 years into the marriage, he had one particular pistol that he kept with him when he was sitting in the living room watching TV. He enjoyed dry firing this gun at random objects in the house, most commonly people on the TV screen.

Mark laid back in his recliner firing his empty pistol. It had become his daily habit. He sat there and pulled the trigger of the unloaded revolver while aiming at the TV, the curio cabinet, pictures on the wall. It's what he did while watching his evening shows.

Beth hated it, but she didn't say much about it. After all, he was a grown man and what business was it of hers what he did?

So, she sat quietly every evening, listening to the periodic dry click of the empty revolver being fired in the living room.

One night, after the kids were in bed, Mark picked up his revolver again. He and Beth were watching TV. She could see him in her peripheral vision lifting the pistol and taking aim at objects in the room like he always did. He wasn't firing the gun, just aiming at stuff. And then she saw him slowly swing the gun in her direction…

She turned to look at him, to look down the barrel of the gun. She couldn't speak. He had never pointed a gun at her before.

As she stared at him, she saw his trigger finger slide into motion.

"Mark, don't!" she pleaded.

He continued to position his finger to pull the trigger.

"Mark, stop! There's a bullet! I see a bullet in the gun!" she screamed.

He laughed.

"No, there's not," he said.

And as his finger reached firing position, she pleaded with him again.

"Mark, don't! Please don't! There's a bullet!"

He held the gun steady and glanced at the pistol while still aiming at his wife.

He saw the gun was loaded.

He slowly lowered it.

Beth was petrified. He was going to shoot her. Mark was going to shoot her. She had pleaded for her life… begged… she had to beg her husband not to shoot her…

Vacation Time

Beth was a simple girl. She liked simple things. She liked being home, but every now and then she got the urge to get out of town. She decided she'd scrimp and save until she had enough money for a trip to Missouri. She wanted to go to a campground not far from Branson. There was no way she could save up enough money to do many touristy things, but they could sightsee in town and relax in the campground. She just wanted to get away for a while.

She worked on saving money for the vacation for two years.

Two years.

When she finally had a few hundred dollars together to cover the cost of gas and camping, she and her little family headed north to their neighboring state.

The trip there was pleasant and uneventful, aside from Mark periodically telling her she wasn't doing a good job of driving. But he complained about her driving every time she was behind the wheel. She was used to it.

As they traveled north, they noticed a sign for a sporting goods store that they had only shopped through catalogs. They decided to stop in and see what the store was like. Mark went his own way, the kids milled around close to their mom, and Beth browsed the coffee mugs. There was one mug in particular that had caught her eye and she couldn't put it down. On one side of the cup was an autumn harvest scene with a tractor and field. On the other side of the mug was a scene with deer. The mug was covered with warm autumn colors. The handle was crafted to look like a cob of corn complete with shucks. It was a beautiful mug.

Eventually Beth put it back on the shelf. It cost $30. Way too much to spend on something pretty when there was still a vacation to pay for.

As they left the store, her oldest son grabbed the mug Beth loved so much. He snuck it to the register and bought it for his mom.

He knew Beth would never spend that kind of money on herself, so he spent it for her.

Her heart was beyond full.

Once they were back in the truck, they resumed their travels northward.

When they arrived at the campground, just across the Arkansas-Missouri border, things took a turn. Mark began belittling Beth. As they set up camp, he spoke down to her, raised his voice to her, and told her she was doing everything wrong. The truth was she was doing nothing wrong. She had set up camp a million times. She knew what to do and how to do it. But Mark wanted her to believe she was less than him, not worth anything, so he verbally beat her.

"I've saved and planned so long for this trip," she thought to herself while she wrangled tent poles, "I'm not going to let him ruin it for the kids and me."

So, she painted on a pretend smile, finished setting up camp, and tried to stay away from Mark.

She kept telling herself over and over, "I just can't let him ruin this trip. I can't let him take this away from me. He's always taking things from me."

She had no idea how bad it was going to get.

After camp was made, Beth and the kids explored the nearby river. The kids seemed to be having a great time.

As they slept in their family-sized tent that night, a strong storm blew in. The walls of the tent vibrated in the wind. Lightning flashed frequently and thunder rumbled. It was an exciting, and slightly scary, way to spend the night.

Eventually the storm passed, and their family was able to sleep. When the sun came up the next morning, their little group crawled out of the tent, one by one, and took in the disarray throughout the campground. Lawn chairs were overturned, tarps had blown away, and tents had collapsed in on themselves. The place was a mess, but all of Beth's and Mark's belongings were intact. She was thankful for that.

After grabbing a bit of breakfast from the cooler, they headed into town to participate in a scenic train ride. When they arrived at the old-fashioned train depot, they noticed a coffee shop across the street. The drive-thru was packed, so Mark told Beth to get out and walk over to the train station to buy their tickets while he and the kids waited in the drive-thru line.

And that's what Beth did. She got out of the truck, walked across the street, and bought the tickets while she waited for the rest of her family to finish up at the coffee shop.

The cashier at the train ticket counter put a mark on one of the tickets. She told Beth that ticket was special. Beth decided to keep the special ticket for herself. Mark had talked so badly to her the day before that she figured she could use the pick-me-up of having the special ticket.

"I wonder what kind of a prize I'll get," she thought.

She didn't tell anyone else about the special ticket.

The train station was very crowded. Beth felt awkward standing in such a crowded place by herself. People were packed into the staging area. Everyone was shoulder to shoulder. She kept raising up on her toes and glancing across the street to see if her family had finished up at the coffee shop. Half an hour had passed, and they were still waiting in line for Mark to get his coffee. Finally, she saw them driving away from the coffee shop. The moment she saw Mark's truck emerge from the drive-thru was the precise moment the train station crowd parted enough for her to see a sign on the depot wall.

The sign said, "No food or drinks allowed on the train."

Her heart sank. She knew Mark would be mad that he couldn't take his coffee on the train. But there was nothing she could do.

Her adrenaline kicked in and she began to shake. He was going to be furious at her.

And he was.

"Why didn't you tell me I couldn't bring my coffee on the train?!"

"Mark, I didn't know," Beth said.

"Beth, you were standing in the train station the whole time I was waiting to get my coffee!'

"I couldn't see the sign, Mark. There were too many people standing in the way."

"There's no way you didn't see that sign! You just wanted me to waste five bucks on a coffee I wouldn't get to drink!"

Beth pleaded with him to believe her, but he blamed the whole situation on her.

He was fuming.

When they boarded the train, she chose not to sit by Mark. She was shaking and wanted to hide her tears from him and the kids. So, she sat by herself next to a window.

The train ride itself was enjoyable. The scenery was pleasant, and the kids especially enjoyed the ride through the tunnel. Then the train slowed and came to a stop while perched on a trestle over a valley. The view was beautiful. It was a long distance from the train to the bottom of the valley below.

The conductor's voice crackled through the loudspeaker.

He said, "If your ticket has a black circle drawn on it, that means you have a special ticket. If you are holding a special ticket, please stand up."

Beth stood up. She was excited to see what prize she would get. She was the only person in their train car to stand.

The conductor spoke again, "Now that you're standing and holding your special ticket, this is what you get. You get… to get off the train. This is your stop. You can jump off the bridge!"

The conductor laughed. The other passengers laughed. But Beth sat back down in her seat and cried, silently and secretly.

After Mark treating her badly for the past 24 hours, the last thing she needed was to hear the conductor tell her to jump off the bridge. So, she sat next to the window and looked outside so her family couldn't see her tears.

She had gotten herself together by the time the ride was over. They stepped off the train, got in their truck, and headed out with Beth behind the wheel.

Family Photo

After the train ride, she wanted to take the kids to a nearby botanical garden that was free to the public. When they got there, Beth and the kids were in awe of how beautiful the scenery was. There were big, gorgeous plants all around, vibrant flowers, and fish ponds next to the walking trails. The tranquility of the gardens was surreal. This type of place wasn't Mark's cup of tea, and he made sure he was grumpy enough that everyone noticed, even strangers passing by. But Beth and the kids were soaking it all in as they walked the winding trails.

As they passed by an especially beautiful array of flowers and leafy plants, Beth told the kids to pose for a picture. A gentleman passing by asked, "Would you like me to take a picture for you so the whole family can be in it?"

"Oh, yes!" Beth said. "That would be awesome!"

She handed her camera to the stranger while Mark grumbled and complained about it. He thought she was stupid for giving her camera to a stranger, and he certainly didn't want to be in a picture.

"Mark, if you don't want to be in the picture, you don't have to," she said.

But he didn't want to be excused that easily, so he posed for the picture too.

When the five of them were ready for the photo, Beth smiled, and the stranger clicked the camera.

"Thank you so much!" she told the man.

"You're welcome!" he said as he smiled and walked away.

Rage Drive

After their excursion to the botanical gardens, they all piled back into the truck.

As Mark started driving, Beth asked, "Where are we going?"

"The sporting goods store," he replied.

Beth didn't have any interest in going to this particular sporting goods store. It was part of a large chain, and she felt like she had been in a million of them over the course of the marriage. But it wouldn't cost anything to go in and look around. And maybe Mark would be happy for a while, so she quietly rode along.

As they were driving down the road something unexpected happened. The oil light came on in the dash panel of the truck. And then the truck started sounding strange. Mark found a place to pull over. He turned off the truck.

"Get out and check the oil," he ordered Beth.

"You've always told me it won't read accurately if the engine is hot," she mentioned.

"Just get out and see what's wrong with the truck!" he barked.

She stepped out as he popped the hood. She carefully pulled out the hot dipstick. It looked like there was plenty of oil.

"The truck has oil," she shouted back toward the cab of the truck. "I don't know what else to check with the engine too hot to touch."

Since it seemed to be okay, they hit the road again.

A couple of miles down the road, the truck started having trouble again.

"What's wrong with my truck?!" Mark shouted.

The gauges on the dashboard had started going crazy. The truck wasn't running well.

With the truck being in a state of chaos, Mark decided the thing to do was to accelerate as hard as possible. He floored it.

"Mark, stop!" Beth pleaded.

Mark didn't listen. He was driving the truck as hard and rough as he could. He was angry. He behaved like a wild man.

"Mark, you're going to blow the engine up!"

He just kept mashing the gas, letting off, and then sinking the pedal to the floor repeatedly.

"Mark, you're going to destroy the truck!" she said.

He sped past a traffic light and into a sharp curve at high velocity.

"Mark, stop it!" Beth cried.

Fast turns and erratic driving had Beth and the kids terrified.

Beth didn't know much about trucks, but she knew he was tearing this one up. She stopped trying to talk sense into him. He was angry. Angry at her because something was wrong with his truck.

"Lord," she quietly prayed, "please keep us safe. And please don't let this truck break down while we're in Missouri. We don't have the money to pay for repairs. How would we ever get back home?"

As they whipped around corners, it took all the courage Beth could muster not to panic. She began to remember a similar situation that had happened in a small town close to home. A man had been angry, his girlfriend, who was in the truck with him, had been terrified and screaming for help as he raced his truck past the courthouse square at extreme speeds. She had such a horrified expression on her face. She begged her boyfriend for mercy. She screamed to bystanders for help. And then he crashed the truck and they both died. It was a horrible memory for Beth to recall in this moment.

Beth and the kids were having a chaotic and wild ride. She was terrified. After many miles of high-speed, reckless driving, they finally made it to the sporting goods store. Beth and the kids were shaken and exited the truck cautiously. Then they all went inside the store.

As they walked past the checkout area, Mark turned and looked at them.

"Well, what do y'all want to look at?!" he raised his voice while throwing his hands in the air.

"Nothing, I guess…" Beth said.

"What?!" Mark raised his voice louder. "You made me drive all the way over here!"

"No, I didn't," Beth said. "I hate this sporting goods store. You were the one who said you wanted to come here."

Mark was getting angrier by the second.

He stomped away. Beth and the kids followed.

They had been in the store for two minutes before they were right back in the truck.

And, in Mark's mind, it was all Beth's fault. It was her fault he had driven all the way to the store. It was her fault that the truck was having problems. It had been her fault that his five-dollar coffee got wasted. It was her fault – all of it. And he made sure to drill that into her mind.

He berated her incessantly after they left the store, until she finally shut down. She went numb. She was left with nothing but a lifeless gaze in her eyes.

She had tried so hard to hang onto joy, to have a vacation filled with wonderful moments. But he won. He always won.

Mark's behavior didn't hurt only her. It hurt the children as well. Even 15 years after that vacation, if she mentioned the trip to Missouri, the kids, who had been adults for quite some time, would groan and say, "Yeah, that was a terrible time."

Beth had worked hard to save the money for that trip. Two years of saving a dollar here, two dollars there. She had been so happy and excited for the vacation.

And Mark destroyed it.

He always destroyed the things she loved.

Worth a Thousand Words

After they got home from their vacation, Beth sent off to have the film from her camera developed. It arrived two weeks later.

As she pulled the family vacation photo out of the envelope, she drew in a ragged breath.

"Oh, God... my kids..."

She gazed at the photo trying to make sense of what she was seeing. The kids' faces showed extreme strain. They had tried to smile, but... her daughter's smile was empty. Her youngest son's smile was... pained. Her oldest son didn't try to smile at all. The children all looked so pale and lifeless.

And Beth... she was smiling in the photo, but her smile was... cold.

Beth wasn't the only one breaking beneath the weight of Mark's behavior. Her kids were breaking too.

And Mark? He had the same dead expression he always had in photos.

Oil Change

A couple of weeks after arriving home from the trip to Missouri, the truck broke down. The engine seized up and was ruined. Mark and Beth got a bank loan and paid to have a new engine put in the truck.

A few months passed and it was time for an oil change. Beth was the one who made sure the oil changes were done, because Mark simply didn't care. If it had been left up to him, none of their vehicles throughout their entire marriage would have ever received an oil change.

During this phase of their lives, Beth was working from home. She was very busy meeting daily deadlines.

Her husband had made a mistake at work and was sent home on a one-week suspension. He was sitting in his recliner watching TV non-stop while Beth was working.

Beth said, "While you're off work, how about you take the truck to town and get the oil changed? It needs to be done, but I'm too busy with work."

"No," he said. "Since I'm missing a week of work, we'd better save money and not get the oil changed."

Mark had never before expressed concern about making ends meet, so Beth found his concern over saving that $60 to be refreshing.

But within two hours of telling her they should wait to get an oil change so they could save that money, he had gone online and spent over $600 on hunting and fishing gear.

"You said we didn't have the money for an oil change," she said. "You don't even need any of the stuff you ordered!"

Mark looked down with a rather sheepish expression. He didn't cancel his orders. He also didn't go get the oil changed.

When he went back to work the following week, he texted Beth.

"I need you to drive to my job and get my truck. Take it for an oil change while I'm at work," he said.

"I can't. I'm working," she told him.

"The truck really needs an oil change," he said.

Beth replied, "It will take me an hour to drive to where you work. It will take me an hour to drive back home. And probably another hour to get the oil changed. You had all last week to get that done. All last week while you were off work."

Beth refused. That was the end of the conversation.

It took courage for her to stand up to him. She didn't know where that courage had come from, but she was so glad it showed up. She had spent the majority of their married life trying to keep Mark from being upset with her. He liked to yell at her, belittle her and punish her in his own little ways. For her to have this moment of courage and stand up to him… was a monumental shift in their relationship.

She was broken.

She was tired.

She was fed up with Mark.

Dust and Deer Lanes

August of each year was the time Mark and Beth worked on their deer hunting spots. Since the prior season, weeds had grown up in their shooting lanes and wasps had built nests in their hunting stands. There was always plenty of work to do to prepare for the upcoming hunt in the fall.

Beth didn't mind the work. She actually enjoyed it. But it was hot, sweaty work and took a lot out of her. Once the shooting lanes had been mowed, and wasps removed from stands, Mark would take his place in the shooter's chair. As he looked from his lofty perch, he would direct Beth as to which tree limbs needed to be trimmed so there would be no obstacles between him and the deer when it came time for the hunt.

Beth would often trim these limbs for him for hours while he sat in the comfortable shade of his hunting stand.

"Let's trade spots," she suggested. "I'm tired of trimming limbs. My arms are getting shaky from working these pruning shears."

"No," he said.

"Why? I can see just as well as you can what needs to be trimmed when I sit in the deer stand," she said.

"No, it has to be what I see in my line of vision. You and I aren't the same height. You wouldn't see my shooting lanes the same way I see them," he said.

She didn't say it out loud, but she was thinking, "Just an excuse for him to sit there and let me do all the work. Like always."

Once the hunting lanes were fully prepared, Mark wanted to go to a different area of the deer lease to plant a food plot. It was in full sun during the hottest hours of the day. The temperature was 104 degrees.

Mark used the four-wheeler to drag a special implement across the ground. The implement stirred up the dirt and made it soft enough for planting. Back and forth he went on the four-wheeler. It was easy work for him. All he was doing was driving.

Beth and the kids had different work to do. The kids had to run in and out of the path of the four-wheeler picking up rocks and sticks from the ground. They had to use rakes and hoes to work the soil. They were doing hard physical labor in the harshest heat of August.

Mark made Beth sit on the implement he was dragging across the ground. He needed her weight on it so it would be heavy enough to properly disturb the dirt. She didn't like it. She felt rather used. But she did it because he demanded it of her.

Back and forth he drove with Beth sitting on the implement. She was covered in dust, which turned to mud in her sweat. The vibration of the implement was jarring, and her whole body was in pain. Sometimes Mark turned the four-wheeler too quickly and Beth was flung off onto the ground, her arms and legs flailing as she tumbled.

Once Mark was finished with the implement, Beth started helping the kids with their work. They were getting overheated, all of them but Mark. She told the kids to go stand in the shade and sip water for a while.

"No," Mark said, "they need to be out here working!"

"No, Mark, they're way too hot and need to cool down. I'll take over for them."

So, Beth raked and hoed and worked the soil.

And then she fell to the ground with the heat of the blazing sun beating against her.

Mark directed the kids to pour some water over her to cool her down.

Once she was able to stand again, they all continued working.

Mark wasn't letting anyone leave until his food plot had been planted.

Deadbeat

Beth didn't mind working. Whether at home or at a job, she liked to be active and productive. It seemed the opposite for Mark. He liked to relax and watch other people work.

One autumn, when they had been married about 25 years, Mark went deer hunting. He called Beth from the woods and told her to bring her truck to him.

"Mark, I'm busy right now."

"Get our son and bring me your truck," he ordered.

So, she and their 16-year-old son got in the truck and headed up to deer camp. When they got there, Mark ordered their son to load up the three deer he had just killed and take them home to clean them.

Three deer. Three deer that were laying in ankle-deep muddy water. Three deer he had killed within five minutes of each other.

Beth questioned him, "Why can't you load up your three deer and go clean them yourself?"

Mark chuckled, "I did the hard part. I killed them."

"Why did you kill three deer all at once??" Beth asked.

"Because I can," he said.

She argued with him for a moment and then she helped their son drag them out of the water and load them in the truck. One of the other hunters from their deer club was there and he helped too. But Mark didn't lift a finger to help. He simply stood and watched. He literally stood and watched as another man stepped in to do what he should have been doing himself.

Beth found it to be pathetic.

"I can't stand being married to him," she thought.

Beth and her son took the deer home. Her child angrily cleaned all three carcasses and Beth assisted as much as she could. The temperature was below freezing, and it was well after midnight by the time the job was finished.

Once the deer were cleaned, she put the meat in a large cooler filled with ice. The cooler sat in the kitchen floor. In normal circumstances, Beth would take the cooler outside once a day and drain the water from the melted ice. Then she'd bring the cooler back into the kitchen and refill it with ice. After repeating the process for three days, the meat would be ready to be cut into slices and frozen.

But this time the situation was a little different than normal. This time Mark had taken time off work. He was home for the first two weeks of deer season. He spent a little of that time at hunting camp, but most of his two-week vacation was spent sitting in his recliner at home and watching TV. He liked to tell people he took off work for the first two weeks of deer season, but he hardly hunted at all during that time. He just stayed at home and watched hour after hour of TV.

Beth continued to work from home. Every day she had strict deadlines to meet.

Considering how busy she was and how not busy her husband was, she chose not to tend to the deer meat in the cooler. Mark wasn't doing anything besides watching TV, so she made sure to remind him there was venison in the cooler that needed to be drained and have fresh ice poured over it.

"Mark, remember there's deer meat that needs to be drained and iced."

"Then do it," he said.

"I'm working," Beth responded.

The next day, "Mark, there's still deer meat in the cooler that needs to be taken care of."

"Then do it," he told her again.

"I'm busy with work. You are the one who chose to kill three deer. You're off work and I'm not. You need to take care of it," she said.

Mark didn't touch the deer meat. He never drained the water, never iced it down. He simply let the meat from the three deer he'd killed sit in room temperature water in the cooler for nine days.

He didn't forget. Beth mentioned it daily. He simply chose not to take the responsibility.

And, so, the meat was ruined. On the ninth day, Beth lugged the heavy cooler outside. She discarded the rotten venison, rinsed the cooler and then scrubbed it with bleach and soap. She did all this while Mark was at deer camp for a few hours.

Though Beth was normally quiet, as Mark walked out the door with his hunting gear earlier that ninth day, she said, "Do NOT kill any more deer."

Mark glanced back over his shoulder, smirked, and left.

When he came home a few hours later, he was empty-handed. Beth was relieved.

He noticed the cooler was gone.

He asked, "Did you cut up the deer meat and put it in the freezer?"

"No," she said. "That meat sat in the cooler in dirty water for nine days. It was spoiled so I threw it out."

He huffed and wagged his head back and forth in frustration.

"There were three deer in that cooler!" he exclaimed.

"Yes, and you chose to watch TV instead of take care of the meat," she calmly responded.

Mark was furious.

So was Beth.

Perpetually Late

Beth put a lot of effort into being a responsible person. She tried very hard to take loving care of the kids, to cook nourishing meals, keep the house clean, and be on time for family events. She put every effort into doing things right.

When Beth was a teen, her family was often late for church and other events. Their frequent tardiness was significant enough that one of the elderly women at church made fun of the family one Sunday by commenting that they were "perpetually late." It was painfully embarrassing for Beth. So, she determined, as an adult, she would never be late for events.

During her marriage to Mark, she worked very hard to always be on time. She was sometimes later than she wanted to be, but 99% of the time Beth was ready to walk out the door on time or even early for family events.

Yet 99% of the time she arrived late. Very, very late.

What happened to cause her to arrive late to family holiday gatherings when she was ready to walk out the door 20 minutes ahead of schedule?

Mark. That's what happened.

He had this thing he did. Whenever Beth and the kids were ready to head to Granny's house for Christmas dinner, or Grandad's house for a July fish fry, Mark would suddenly decide one of the kids had stolen something that belonged to him. One time it was a flashlight, another time it was an empty canister. It could be anything and everything. He always noticed his belongings had been "stolen" precisely when it was time for their little family to pile into the car. And it was always an item he didn't need in that moment.

"Where's my pocket saw?" he asked.

"I don't know. Where did you have it last?" Beth responded.

"It was in my backpack that I take to the woods and now it's gone. One of the kids stole it!"

"Mark, nobody stole your saw. It's around here somewhere," she said. "We can look for it after we get back from having Christmas dinner with my Mom."

"No! I want everyone looking for it right now! Nobody leaves until it's found!" he shouted.

Beth and the kids scoured the house for an hour.

"Mark, are you sure it's not in your hunting backpack?" Beth asked. She was sick of looking for it. And they were now incredibly late for dinner.

"Yes, I looked! It's not in there!" he shouted.

"Well, we've searched the house and the truck and haven't found it. I'm going to doublecheck your backpack," Beth said.

"I already looked and it's not in there!" he shouted.

"Mark, it's not anywhere else we've looked. It won't hurt to check your backpack a second time."

So, Beth searched every pocket and crevice in his hunting pack. And she found the foldable saw they'd been searching for.

"I found it. It's in your backpack," she said. "Can we leave for Christmas dinner at Mom's now?"

And, so, he would accuse his kids of stealing whatever item it was, and he would force everyone to search for the item until it was found. This insanity resulted in their late arrival for… everything. 30 minutes late, an hour late, and sometimes they didn't show up for the event at all. It was incredibly frustrating for the kids and infuriating for Beth.

After years of being late for family gatherings and other events, Beth's extended family started to make fun of her.

"We knew you'd be late," they would say. "You're never on time. We thought we were going to starve just waiting for you to get here for dinner."

Or, "We knew you'd never be on time so we went ahead and ate Christmas dinner without you."

It stung deeply. They teased her in a loving way, assuming it was her fault she was always late. No one had any idea of what Beth and the kids had to endure to even be present.

The one thing that Beth told herself as a child she would never do as an adult turned out to be something that was out of her control. And she was made fun of for it.

Beth could handle a lot of things. But it cut her to the core to be mocked and made fun of.

Days and Hours

Beth started a new job. It was in a field of work that involved disgruntled, dangerous people. Her work was part-time, which worked out perfectly. One of their children had developed a health issue, and sometimes he had medical appointments that Beth would take him to. It would have been difficult to work full-time and make all the doctor's appointments.

She had been working at her new job for several weeks, and Mark had no idea of what days and hours she worked. She always left for work after he did, and she arrived home before him.

"My job is a little dangerous. I need to tell you what days I work so you'll know to check on me if I don't come home on time," she said.

"I don't care," he replied.

"You don't care?" she asked. "You don't want to know what days and hours I'm at work?"

"Nope," he responded.

Gaslighting

"I think he's gaslighting you," Beth's sister said.

"What's gaslighting?" Beth asked. It was the first time she'd ever heard such an odd term.

"Look it up online," Sassy instructed.

Beth was astounded by what she learned. In the most basic terms, gaslighting is when someone repeatedly and methodically lies to their victim, causing the victim to lose their perception of reality over time. In essence, it's artificially-induced insanity.

For Beth and Mark, it went something like this:

"Hey, Beth, why is there no water in the coffee maker?"

"I guess because you used it all making coffee," she'd respond.

"I told you it needed to be refilled as I was leaving for work this morning!" he'd say.

"No, you didn't…"

"Beth! You don't listen to a word I say! I told you it was empty when I filled my thermos this morning! I told you to put more water in it!" he'd shout.

"Mark… no, you didn't. You didn't say anything to me about putting water in the coffee maker…" she'd tell him.

"Nobody listens to me!" he'd shout.

Or it might be a scenario like, "Hey, Beth, did you get all the trash out of the cab of my truck yet?"

"No, was I supposed to?"

"I told you yesterday that I needed you to clean out my truck! Oh my gosh, you don't listen to me at all!"

In reality, he'd never asked her to do any of those things. But he made her think he had asked her to. He made her think she had failed him.

She had lived with Mark for 25 years before she had heard the term gaslighting. Once she started researching it, the pieces of the puzzle began to fit together. Mark gaslit her at least once a week, sometimes more. Over a period of 25 years, Mark's efforts to make her feel insane had begun to work.

During the course of the marriage, he had manipulated her into thinking she was forgetful, she had failed at something, she was stupid, over 1,300 times.

She questioned herself constantly. She made intense effort to listen to every word he said so she wouldn't miss anything or forget, and yet, somehow, he was always telling her she had forgotten what he'd told her.

After years of being psychologically manhandled, he had manipulated her to the point that she had begun to believe she was insane. She literally thought she had early onset dementia.

But when she learned about gaslighting, she realized maybe she wasn't the person with the problem.

"Beth, did the pharmacy have all of my prescriptions ready today?" Mark asked.

"What do you mean?" she responded.

"Did you pick up all three of my meds?" he said.

"I didn't go to the pharmacy. I didn't know you wanted me to," Beth said.

"Beth! I told you this morning to go to the pharmacy! I stood right here by my chair and told you to go get those medicines for me because I'm out of them! Do I need to write it on a sticky note and slap it on your forehead??"

"No, Mark," she calmly said as she took a slow, deep breath, "you didn't. You didn't say anything at all to me about this. Maybe you thought about it, but you never actually said it to me."

With the new knowledge she had, she'd caught him in the act. He tried to gaslight her, and she called him out on it. He went quiet. He had no response.

After 25 years of mental manipulation, she had turned the tables. She felt an incredible weight lift from her in that moment. She smiled. She couldn't stop smiling.

"I'm not crazy after all," she told herself. "I'm not crazy… I'm not crazy…"

It was a moment of victory. A moment she desperately needed.

Lies, Lies, Lies

Once she learned what gaslighting was, she thought back over their years together. In the course of the marriage, Beth learned that Mark had lied to her a couple of times while they had been dating. They weren't major lies, but he had told her things that were false, and she had believed him. He once told her a very detailed story of how he and his friend had seen a ball of fire hovering over a field. Beth tossed around ideas of what it could have been. She took it seriously and tried to help him figure out what it was. For years, she remembered the story he'd told her. One day, years after the fact, she mentioned it in conversation. He laughed at her and told her he'd made that story up. It was a lie.

"I can't believe you believed that story!" he laughed.

He had lied, fed her a completely false story, and let her believe it for years and years.

Beth felt betrayed. She felt stupid for believing him.

On another occasion, during the months they dated, he told her he'd quit smoking. He said he had quit cold turkey. He told her he had smoked a whole pack of cigarettes one right after another until it made him sick, and he never wanted to see another cigarette again.

She was so proud of him! Beth was a supportive, encouraging person. She told him what a great job he was doing.

A couple of weekends after he stopped smoking, she went to visit him at his grandparents' house. Several members of his family were there. Beth was generally a quiet person, but she decided to speak up and tell his family how proud she was of Mark.

"I am so happy for him that he's quit smoking! It's not an easy thing to do. I'm so proud of him!" she had said.

No one in the room spoke. They looked at her like… she was crazy. She glanced at

Mark who was looking around at everyone rather sheepishly. Beth was stunned by the silence.

"Well, I'm proud of him…," she quietly said.

After they were married, she noticed he started smoking again. That's when he admitted he had never actually stopped smoking. He had lied to her about it.

"Why would you lie to me about that? You made me look like a fool in front of your family!" she said.

"I didn't think you'd marry me if I didn't quit smoking," he responded.

"I never said anything to make you think that. Of course, I was going to marry you whether you smoked or not."

He had also lied to her about his taste in music. She even bought him an album as a gift when they were dating because he told her he liked music by that artist. Then he told her, years later, that he had lied about that too.

"Why would you lie to me about that?" Beth asked.

"I didn't think you'd marry me if I liked a different kind of music than you did."

Finding out about the lies, even though they were little, made her wonder what else he had lied about. And it made her question why he did it. What was the point?

Honestly, she began to feel as though he had manipulated her into loving him, tricked her into marrying him. She realized that was an extreme thought, but as the marriage had progressed, a lot of things in the relationship turned out to be extreme. Being deceived into marrying him really wasn't such a far-fetched theory.

Once they reached the 25-year point of marriage, she began to wonder why he had felt the need to marry her, to manipulate her into marriage. All she could come up with was maybe marrying her was a step up for him. Maybe he wanted to show his neglectful, low-income family that he could marry into a good, middle-class family, that he could be accepted by a good girl. Beth and her family were known in the community and relatively well liked. Maybe he felt there was prestige to be gained from marrying her.

"I don't even know who I married…" she whispered to herself.

Mark the Narc

"He's such a narcissistic butt," Sassy said.

"What on earth is a narciss... narcissis... what did you say?" Beth struggled.

"Narcissist," Sassy replied. "You can learn all about it online. I believe that's what Mark is, or at least it seems like what his problem is."

So, Beth delved into research about narcissism. She talked with people who had knowledge on the topic, she read articles, she searched websites. She didn't have a clue what it was, so she dug in everywhere she could.

Her friend sent her a list of traits common to narcissists.

"Hmmm... narcissistic personality disorder..." she read.

'~A sense of self-importance'

"Well, that definitely fits Mark. He's the most important person in his world. And everything revolves around him and what he wants…"

'~Entitled'

"Oh, yeah, that's definitely Mark. He feels like everyone owes him something."

'~Arrogant'

"Oh, boy! That's definitely him! I've never met anyone more arrogant than my husband."

'~Lack of empathy for others'

"Wow… these are all spot on…"

'~Controlling behavior, need for grandiosity and attention, demeans and bullies others, gaslighting…'

"He's a narcissist! He has almost every quality of narcissistic personality disorder. Almost every single one!" Beth thought. "At least I have some knowledge now, some knowledge of why he's such a mean-spirited, horrible person…"

She texted Sassy, "You're right! He's a narcissist!"

"I don't think he's necessarily a full-blown narcissist, but he's definitely got some of the qualities," Sassy replied.

"I think he's full-blown narc. Listen to these traits."

Beth listed several characteristics of narcissists.

"There's more to it but look at all of the symptoms he has!"

Beth was convinced Mark was a narcissist to the highest level. It explained a lot. Actually, it explained everything.

"I feel bad for him," she thought. "He can't help it."

And then she realized he's fully aware of every hurtful thing he does. He acts with malice and anger in his heart.

"Narcissism explains why he acts the way he does, but it excuses nothing. I don't deserve to be treated like a dog."

College Days

"I want to go to trade school, Beth. I want to make something of myself. I want to learn to weld. Welders are making a lot of money these days," he said.

"I'd love for you to be able to do that," she replied. "But how will we pay our bills if you're in school?"

"Oh, I'll keep working and go to school too. I can work evening shift and we won't lose any income."

He started trade school a few weeks later. He was working at a boat factory at the time, working in the evenings and going to school during the day. It was a lot to balance.

He finally decided there was no way he could do both.

"I need to quit my job so I can focus on school," he told her.

"Ummm… how will we pay our bills if you're not working?"

"It'll be fine. I'm sure your income will be enough to pay the bills," was his response.

"Mark, we can't make it on just my income. You've got to keep working too. There's no way we can make it on my income."

"Look, you take care of the bills while I go to school. It's just a nine-month program and then I'll be done and have my welding certifications. After that, I will work so you can go to school. Sound good?" he proposed.

"Mark… I don't think we can do this. There's no way we can pay all our bills with just the money I earn," Beth replied.

"It's the way it's going to have to be, Beth," he said. "I can't keep working and going to school too. But, I promise, as soon as I get finished with school, I'll get a good job that will pay the bills, and then you can have your turn in college."

Beth's job wasn't enough, and she knew it. She ended up taking on a second job just to make ends meet.

But she was proud of Mark. He earned honors during his months in the welding program. He graduated with a high GPA. He proudly wore his cap, gown, and honors sash as he crossed the stage on graduation day and accepted his diploma.

Once he settled into a new job with his freshly-earned certifications, she told him, "I've decided what I want to earn a degree in. I want to go to college to become a forester. I love being in the woods, and I especially like dealing with trees. It's the perfect job for me."

"Beth," he shook his head, "we can't afford for you to go to college."

"I'll get financial aid like you did," she said.

"No, I mean you have to keep working. I can't support us with just my job," he told her.

"But you said it would be my turn after you graduated," she reminded him.

"That doesn't matter now. We have bills to pay," he said. "Besides that, no one will respect you as a forester. It's a man's job. All the people you'd be working with are men. No one would listen to you. Nobody would respect you at all."

"This is what I want to do though," she said. "I worked two jobs so we could pay our bills while you were in school. You can do the same thing for me."

"You know, it doesn't even matter about the money anyway. You'll get absolutely zero respect from the loggers and other foresters. Forget it, Beth. This is a man's world."

As reality hit, Beth ached. She knew she'd never get to go to school. She knew he would never support her in that. She knew he lied.

Again.

She thought about her dreams. She'd always had such big hopes for her life. Now she knew her dreams would never be realized.

Not while she was tied to Mark.

The longer she lived with this man who kept her beneath his feet, the deeper she felt the pain of her marriage. It was like what she used to read in old Westerns when the cowboys found themselves in beds of lava rock. With each step they took, the rocks cut deeper and deeper into their boots, until their feet were a bloody mess.

That's how Beth was beginning to feel. Like every step tore her apart a little more.

Four-Wheeler

It was a steamy summer day in the backwoods of Arkansas. Mark, Beth and the kids had gone to put out corn for the deer in their hunting spot. They had one four-wheeler, so all five of them piled on. It was a sight to behold. And it was terribly uncomfortable.

On their way into the woods, they had discovered a yellow jackets' nest. The angry stinging insects were buzzing in and out of their nest in the ground. The yellow jackets of south Arkansas are not to be toyed with. If one attacks, they all attack.

When it was time to leave the woods and come back across the nest, Mark came up with a plan to keep from disturbing the insects. He and the kids would walk quietly past the nest and across the narrow four-wheeler bridge a few yards away. Once they were safely across the creek, Beth would drive the four-wheeler across. She would have to drive directly over the top of the nest and cross the narrow bridge while holding an empty five-gallon bucket and driving a machine with no brakes.

Driving across the nest didn't worry her as much as crossing the bridge did. The bridge was incredibly narrow, and the ATV tires had to line up precisely with the boards across the creek. There was zero room for error.

With husband and children awaiting her arrival on the other side of the creek, Beth started driving. She gained speed quickly and flew over the yellow jackets. Mission one was accomplished.

She lined up the wheels for the rapid creek crossing as she sped down the path. And then the situation hit a snag.

The bucket she'd had perched on her leg had bounced around and gotten wedged between her thigh and the handlebar. Not only could she no longer steer the four-wheeler, the bucket was also wedged against the throttle. She was flying down the path and couldn't slow down.

She tried to dislodge the bucket, but it wouldn't budge. She was going too fast for the bridge crossing. Entirely too fast. She wasn't able to get the wheels lined up.

She couldn't bail off. She was stuck. The wedged bucket had her pinned to the four-wheeler.

This was it. She was going to hit the bridge at a high rate of speed.

And she did.

The four-wheeler's front left wheel went over the side of the bridge. Then the back left wheel. Beth and the vehicle were violently thrown off the side of the bridge. But the four-wheeler didn't entirely fall off the bridge, nor did Beth entirely fall off the four-wheeler. The ATV was hanging off the side of the bridge. The wheels on the right side had caught. The machine was no longer moving, but resting, hanging perpendicular to the bridge.

Beth still had her right leg over the four-wheeler. The wedged bucket still had her stuck. Her left leg was off the four-wheeler and standing on a log in the water. The water level was low that day, so the log was dry and sturdily perched in the creek.

Beth was pushing against the four-wheeler with all her might. She didn't want it to fall. Because if it fell, she would be pinned under it in the water.

She was injured. When the four-wheeler was flung off the side of the bridge, her leg was jabbed by a blunt stob sticking up from the log she was standing on. The pain was great, but she couldn't focus on that. She was still trying not to die.

She screamed for help. She glanced over where Mark and the kids were standing. The kids' faces… those poor babies had just seen their momma wreck. They were terrified. And what they saw next was their daddy yelling at their mom.

As Mark slowly ambled toward her, he rolled his eyes, wagged his head back and forth, and yelled, "You're tearing up my four-wheeler!"

Empty Nest

After all the kids were grown and had moved out, Beth found the silence of the house to be unbearable. She had just started a new job, one that would set the stage to alter the course of her life, and within the following two weeks, she became an empty nester. The change was devastating.

Every day she came home from work, slipped on a black hoodie, put the hood on her head, and curled up in a chair.

The house was silent, aside from the TV which Mark always had on. He had never made an effort to engage in conversation with her, but she'd always had the chatter of the kids to distract her. Now that their house was devoid of that chatter, Beth found the silence to be stifling.

She felt as though she was suffocating to death in her own house.

As she sat encloaked in that black hoodie every day, Mark never said a word.

Evening after evening, nothing from Mark. Just silence.

No Good Memories

25 years after their wedding day, she flipped back through the pages of her memories. Logic dictates there should be good memories, tons of good memories over the course of 25 years, but she couldn't see them. She searched the recesses of her mind, but she had no good memories. If they existed, they were being overshadowed by the memories that hurt. The lack of happy memories weighed heavily on her spirit.

"How can I have a marriage with no happy moments, no good memories?"

Sex Schedule

He said it quite simply, "I'm not interested in sex anymore."

She was stunned. Speechless. Literally speechless.

Early in the marriage, Mark had told Beth he didn't want to have sex very often. She had learned to live with that. But here they were in their mid-30s, and Mark told his wife he wasn't interested in sex anymore. At all.

She felt as though she had nothing left. No more fight in that moment. No more desire to try to keep the bond. She felt utterly and entirely empty.

In the silence that fell after Mark's cold announcement, the bony fingers of defeat began to take hold of her soul.

Days went by. She continued to put one foot in front of the other, trudging through life with an empty smile on her face. There was nothing more than that she could do.

A few weeks after his no-more-sex announcement, he told her he would allow her to have sex, but only on Saturday mornings before he got out of bed. She wouldn't be allowed to have sex any other time.

So, at the age of 35, her husband restricted her to a sex schedule. Three times a month she was allowed to have sex. Three times and no more. Week four was her period, so sex was off the table during that time.

"I don't understand what's happening…" she thought. "Is there something wrong with me? How can a man his age have no interest in sex? I don't understand…"

She tried hard to act as though it didn't hurt her.

But it did.

It was devastating.

Her love for him was waning. It had been in decline for a while, but the loss of connection she felt toward Mark was accelerating. She didn't feel like she had any fight left in her, any fight to try to keep a bond between them. But she forced herself to try anyway. Over time she tried to counter his lack of desire, tried to seduce him, told him she'd be waiting naked in bed for him, even sat on his lap nude but he wouldn't touch her.

The sex schedule lasted for an entire decade.

Beth loved sex. Although there was no passion with Mark, she enjoyed the physical contact. She thrived on physical touch, and since he wouldn't give her significant physical contact in any other way, she enjoyed all the contact she could get in the bedroom.

Even after he put her on a schedule that restricted her to receiving sex only three times a month, she eagerly accepted that physical time together.

She was starved for it.

As much as she loved sex, there were times when it hurt. With every sex session being premeditated, with no spontaneity involved, there was no passion in the bedroom to get her warmed up. Sometimes their time together could be painful.

In the beginning, she'd tell him if he was hurting her.

"Ouch," she would say as she scooted away from him on the bed.

His response was to mock her, to make fun of her.

"Ouch," he would say in a high-pitched, whiny voice.

And if he wasn't mocking her when he hurt her, he was getting angry at her because she told him it hurt. So, Beth learned not to say anything. Over time, she trained herself to go numb to the pain, to be limp and lifeless, to dissociate from reality. Sometimes she would switch it up and focus on the mental image of a beach with warm sand and a soothing breeze. These coping mechanisms helped her get through the pain. She knew Mark wasn't trying to hurt her – it was purely accidental – but she learned to keep the pain to herself.

Physical pain she could endure. Emotional pain she couldn't handle.

After ten years of living by his sex schedule, he finally stopped putting out at all.

Deer Hunting Comes First

Beth knew it was normal for a man's libido to drop over time. She also knew there were medicines to counter it.

As they sat on the front porch together, while Mark smoked his pipe, Beth cautiously asked, "Would you go to the doctor and see if there's something we can do about your sex drive? Sometimes the medicines we take can cause problems in that department. Maybe it's something simple like that. Maybe your blood pressure medicine is causing it."

Beth knew it was a sensitive subject, so she presented her request as gently as she could.

Mark chuckled, "No, I'm not using one of my vacation days for that. I'm saving them for deer season."

"It's just one day," she said carefully. "You have three weeks of vacation time this year. And you know you don't really hunt when you take off work for deer season. You just tell people you're hunting, while you're actually sitting at home watching TV," Beth said. She knew it was a little bold to mention these things to him, but she said it carefully and with as much love as she could muster.

"Yeah, I'm not using a vacation day to go to the doctor," he said.

She had asked him to go to the doctor and see if there was something that could be done to stimulate his sex drive, but he refused. He told her he wanted to use his vacation days from work to go deer hunting later in the year. He didn't want to use a vacation day to go to the doctor. He had three full weeks of vacation time, but he didn't want to use a single day to make sure he was sexually satisfying his wife.

It was in that moment that reality fully sunk in. She held no importance to him.

"He doesn't care about me at all. Not at all…"

As the rose-colored glasses of her love clattered to the ground, an unforgiveable chain of events began to develop on the horizon of her life.

Ordered to Cheat

At some point during the 10 years of the sex schedule, Mark had told her a husband had no excuse to not take care of his woman. He told her if he ever wasn't taking care of her in bed that he was ordering her to cheat. She got angry with him, and they argued. She said that was the most ridiculous thing she'd ever heard. But he insisted, even though she knew he would never expect her to do it. She was a good girl. She'd never cross that line.

But once a woman has been broken, she's capable of anything.

A Time for Truth

"Mark, would you be willing to try marriage counseling with me?"

She was afraid to ask, afraid of how he'd respond.

"Yeah, we can go," he said.

He wasn't enthusiastic about it, but he'd said yes. Beth was shocked.

She made arrangements to see the marriage counselor after she and Mark got off work one day the following week.

As they sat in the room with the counselor, Beth wept. The counselor asked many questions that dug deep into Beth's soul. They were good questions, important questions.

Beth answered honestly. So did Mark.

Then the counselor asked, "Beth, who do you talk with when you have a problem? Who do you confide in?"

Beth was quiet for a long time as she tried to think of who she talked to.

Finally, she said, "Nobody. Well, sometimes I talk with my sister, but normally I don't talk to anyone about my problems."

The counselor asked, "You don't talk with Mark about your problems?"

"Oh, no," Beth said. "I don't."

"Why not?" the counselor asked.

"Because he doesn't want to hear about my problems," Beth replied. To hear those words come out of her mouth so quickly caught her by surprise. She had always known it in her heart, but she had never before put that sentiment into words.

The counselor turned to Mark, "Is this true? You don't want Beth to talk with you about her problems?"

"No, I don't want to know about her problems," Mark said.

Then he smiled.

Like A Puppet on a String

Ever since she had become an empty nester, Beth had begged Mark to put some effort into their relationship. He wouldn't do it. He simply didn't care. For months she begged. For months he did nothing at all about it.

She had gotten to the point where she had nothing left to give their marriage. She was empty, completely drained. So, she left Mark for a couple of weeks during deer season. She told him she needed a vacation too, just like he did, so she was going to stay at her dad's house while Mark took his two-week hunting vacation. He texted while Beth was away.

"Look, Beth, I know our marriage is on the rocks, but we can't work it out if you aren't here. Come home so we can work things out."

After months of putting zero effort into their marriage, Beth was shocked that he wanted to try.

"He wants to work on our marriage? Finally?" Beth thought. "Wow… this is good. Very good!"

She gathered up a handful of the things she had taken to her dad's and drove back home so she and Mark could talk. She was smiling. She couldn't help it. He finally wanted to work on their marriage. She walked into their house, put her things down, and then sat in a chair close to where Mark was sitting. She looked at him expectantly, thinking maybe he had something specific he wanted to say. But he didn't say anything. He stared at the TV.

Then he picked up the remote, clicked the TV off, and started to walk toward the bedroom.

"Where are you going?" Beth asked.

"I'm going to bed," he said.

"I thought we were going to talk," Beth replied.

"Look, I know our marriage is in bad shape, but I have to get up early tomorrow. It's my bedtime."

As he walked away, Beth began to cry.

"What is it now?!" he yelled.

She just shook her head. He walked away.

She thought about going back to her dad's house but decided to sleep in Mark's recliner that night. She cried herself to sleep.

Sometime during the night, Mark came skulking into the living room. In the darkness, she could see him looking around. Then he huffed and walked back to the bedroom. She heard the bed creak as he crawled back in.

She got up and went to the guest bathroom. He must have heard the toilet flush, because a few seconds later he came back into the living room and realized she had curled up in his recliner.

In the silence of the night, he screamed, "What are you doing??!"

Beth was scared of him in that moment.

"I'm sleeping," she quietly said.

He stomped back to the bedroom and slammed the door.

The next morning, he stormed out of the house. Beth was following him trying to talk with him. He slammed the door in her face.

It wasn't the first time he had shut a door in her face. Actually, he always shut the door in her face. If they were entering a store, walking into a restaurant, going over to her mother's for a holiday dinner, Mark always walked in the door first and let the door slam in her face. She was used to it. But this time he slammed the door so hard it made the whole house shake.

After his truck roared out of the driveway, she went to the bathroom and turned on the shower. She took off her sweats, stepped into the warm shower, and she screamed. And screamed. And screamed.

She pounded her fists against the shower wall and cried and screamed some more.

"Why?!!!!!" she screamed. "Why?!!!! Why?!!!!"

She stood in the streaming hot water and cried until her eyes were swollen and she could barely breathe. Then she got out, dried off, dressed herself and went back to her dad's.

After the two-week break, she came back home to Mark. Their relationship stayed the same.

Eventually she left Mark for three months, but she came back to him again. She was determined to make their marriage work. He wasn't putting any effort into making the relationship better after she came back home, but Beth was determined to be satisfied with life no matter what came her way. At least now, after her being gone for three months, he seemed to be a nicer person.

Beth tried to be happy, or at least content in the marriage, but she simply wasn't. She was empty. She was suicidal. It was a feeling that came around periodically for her, but she never told anyone. She had certainly never told Mark. It was her own personal darkness, and she silently lived with it.

But this time she decided to try talking with Mark. He was her husband. He was supposed to be the person who loved her and supported her no matter what.

So, she quietly told him about her depression as he sat in his recliner watching TV.

"Mark, I'm feeling really low… I don't feel like living anymore."

She looked pleadingly at him.

He rolled his eyes.

"I don't care," he said.

An Apology for the Records

Beth and the kids, who had all grown into adults and were living on their own, decided to make a family outing to the top of a local mountain. Some of the kids' friends would participate too. The mountain was barely tall enough to be classified as an official mountain, and tons of people hiked it daily. An athletic person could easily reach the peak and be back to the bottom of the mountain in around an hour. A hearty hike for people like Beth and Mark, but nothing impossible.

Their group had a bible lesson planned for their time at the peak. Kind of a sermon on the mount. Everyone was looking forward to it. Everyone except Mark.

"Why do we have to do something hard? Why can't we all do something I want to do?" he complained.

"Because you're the only one who doesn't want to do the hike. And you don't have to if you don't want to," Beth said.

So, all of the family and friends met together at the base of the mountain early one Sunday, even Mark.

The little group trudged over the rocky trail. The youngest of the pack was in the lead. Beth and Mark brought up the rear.

"I've gone as far as I can," Mark said.

"Ok," Beth said. "There's a bench just a few steps farther. You can rest there while the rest of us finish the hike."

She felt bad for abandoning him, but she didn't want to miss out on time with her kids, so she kept going.

They had a wonderful time at the top of the mountain. It was a hot day, but there were a few trees providing cool shade, and there was a gentle breeze stirring. One of the kids' friends read from the Bible and everyone had prayer time. There was lots of laughter and camaraderie amongst the group in that moment.

After an hour at the peak, they slowly picked their way back down the trail. Mark was still sitting on the bench. He rejoined the group as they made their way to the base of the hill.

Once they reached the bottom, everyone said their goodbyes and went in separate directions.

Mark and Beth slowly walked toward their truck.

They were surrounded by a beautiful park with lots of families playing games and having picnics. There was a small kayaking stream along the edge of the mountain property.

As they walked, Beth noticed a husband and wife preparing to unload their canoe at the stream. The man was standing outside the truck. The wife was behind the steering wheel.

"Back the truck all the way to the stream!" he shouted at her.

"Ok," she said, "but I need to go to the bathroom first."

She began to drive the truck in the direction of the public restrooms.

"What are you doing?!" her husband screamed.

"I need to use the bathroom," she said.

"No, you back that truck up to the stream right now! I don't care if you need to use the bathroom! That's not why we're here! Back up the truck!"

Beth didn't say anything. She and Mark just kept on walking. But her heart was screaming in pain for that woman. And it was screaming in pain for herself.

"Oh…" she thought, "that sounds just like the way Mark talks to me."

They continued to walk in silence.

And then Mark spoke.

"I'm sorry," he said.

"What for?" she asked.

"I'm sorry I ever talked to you like that man just talked to his wife."

It was only the second time she'd ever received a sincere apology from him. She was completely taken by surprise.

They walked a few more steps in silence.

"Thank you," Beth said. "I was thinking about those moments with you when I heard that man yelling at his wife… thank you for apologizing."

Just a short couple of weeks later, they made a trip to the lake. And although his words were sincere in the moment, they meant nothing after the lake trip.

Apology, Null and Void

Mark decided he and Beth should make a trip to the lake. It was about a two-and-a-half-hour drive. Beth drove the whole way. Mark was quite pleasant during the drive. Noticeably pleasant. Beth found herself enjoying his company, and it surprised her. It was the first time in 25 years of marriage that she could remember truly enjoying being in the vehicle with him.

As they neared the lake, Beth needed to pee. After all, they had been on the road for two-and-a-half hours, so it was definitely time for a potty break. They were in a secluded, rural area, so Beth pulled the truck down a side road and stepped out to use the bathroom. When she got back in the truck a minute later, she could feel the change in the atmosphere. Mark was angry. Very angry. He didn't speak, but she could feel it.

Beth had become adept at reading the atmosphere around Mark. It was a survival skill she had learned over the years.

Before she had stopped to use the bathroom, he was in a great mood. After she had used the bathroom, his anger filled the cab of the truck like a dark, ugly cloud.

It puzzled Beth.

They got to the lake just a few minutes later. Mark was still mad. Beth parked the truck near the bank of the lake. She was a bit taller than Mark, so once they had the canoe unstrapped from the top of the truck, she reached up and began the process of pulling it to unload. Once the canoe tipped toward the ground, Mark grabbed it and started pulling. He pulled hard. It came off the truck much too quickly and fell on top of Beth. Mark could have prevented it from falling on her, but he didn't. He didn't care if it fell on Beth. It almost seemed as if he wanted the boat to fall on her.

"Did he do that intentionally?" she asked herself. "It really seems like he did…"

He didn't ask if she was ok. All he did was huff in aggravation.

She wasn't hurt. Not too much. So, she lifted it off of her head and helped carry it to the lake.

"Why on earth is he mad at me?" she thought. "All I did was stop the truck for a potty break."

They planned to camp on an island at the lake, so there were a lot of supplies to unload. She and Mark carried the camping gear from the truck. She placed the items she got out of the truck next to the canoe at the edge of the water. Piece by piece, she carried gear and set it down. Mark was arranging gear inside the canoe.

After several minutes of nothing but silence, he yelled at her, "Why aren't you putting the gear in the canoe?! Why are you putting it on the ground?!"

Beth was taken aback, but only slightly. Nothing really surprised her with Mark anymore.

"I'm putting it next to the canoe so you can arrange the gear the way you like it. You don't like the way I load gear into the canoe," she said. "And if you're going to act like that, we can just turn right around and go home."

"Wow! Where did that come from?" she thought.

She stood up for herself! She had gotten tired enough of his horrible attitude toward her that she stood up for herself! It felt good!

Apparently, Beth speaking up for herself was exactly the medicine he needed. He shut up and his attitude changed for the better.

But his about-face made her wonder if he had mental problems. It was as though a switch had flipped in his brain when she stopped on the way to the lake to pee. She hadn't done anything to upset him. She simply pulled onto an isolated rural road and used the bathroom. But in the two minutes it took to stop the truck, pee, and get back in, he had become a whole different person.

"That doesn't even make sense," she thought. "It's like he's two people. There's a nice version, which apparently reaches its limit at two-and-a-half hours, and there's the mean version of Mark. And the mean version is the one that usually comes out to play."

"I just don't understand him…" she thought.

Hitting Rock Bottom

Weeks passed and Mark decided he wanted to take Beth on a float trip on one of the cold-water rivers in the northern part of the state. Beth was apprehensive about being stuck in a canoe with him for hours, but she agreed. Mark meant it to be a time of bonding between them. A time to refresh their relationship. That's how he pitched the idea anyway. Floating a river together is a fun adventure. Or at least it should be.

The morning was beautiful. The first few minutes of the float were peaceful and relaxing. There was a cool fog rolling across the water. It was lovely.

Then they came to a section of river where the water was very shallow, and the canoe got stuck on the gravel riverbed. The water was only a couple of inches deep in this spot. Beth put one of her legs over the side of the canoe and began to push off the gravel bottom with her foot. Mark yelled at her.

"Get your foot back in the canoe!"

"I'm just trying to get the boat moving again."

But every time she tried to put her leg over to push, he yelled at her.

He was using his paddle to push against the river bottom, but the canoe wasn't budging at all. Every time either of them moved, she could hear the rocky riverbed grinding against the bottom of the boat.

"Let's just get out of the boat and get away from this shallow spot," Beth said as she began to get out of the canoe.

"Sit down! Don't you dare step out of this canoe!" Mark yelled.

So, she sat there, on the middle seat of the canoe, feeling like an idiot while Mark shoved with his paddle and tried to move the boat by shifting his body weight.

Two fishermen standing at the edge of the water were watching Beth and Mark.

They started to walk out and help, but Mark told them not to.

She was embarrassed more than she had ever been embarrassed in her life.

After 20 minutes of struggling with the canoe, it finally drifted free. The embarrassment of having fishermen witness Mark talking down to her, the embarrassment of having them try to help and Mark telling them no, had ruined the trip for her.

Mark ignored her the rest of the float, and that was okay with her. She didn't want to talk to him anyway.

She kept her head turned away from Mark and let the cool breeze of the morning dry the tears on her face.

Passport

"I want to take a vacation to The Bahamas," he told her. A few weeks had passed since the float trip, and he was pitching the idea of a tropical vacation. Beth wasn't interested in going to The Bahamas, but she didn't tell him that. She figured if he wanted to spend his pocket money to take her on a vacation, she would absolutely go and try to enjoy it.

"I need you to find a post office that does passports and the passport photos too. Get us an appointment for a Friday," Mark told her.

She went online and found a post office that took care of passport applications and photos on site. She made an appointment for the following Friday.

Mark took the day off work, and the two of them made the drive to their capital city. As they pulled into the post office parking lot, Beth began to get anxious.

"Oh, God," she prayed, "please make this be the post office that does photos. If I made a mistake, Mark will yell at me."

And then she saw the sign, "Passport photos taken here."

"Whew!" she prayed again, "thank you, Lord!"

They went inside and signed in for their appointment. As they waited to be called into the passport room, Beth felt a bit of excitement. She looked around at all the vacation signs and posters encouraging people to travel the world. She was about to apply for her very first passport! She knew she had a stupid smile on her face, but she couldn't help it. She was excited!

After an hour of waiting, the passport clerk asked when their appointment time was. Beth told him.

"I'm afraid you have the wrong date," he said. "Your appointment isn't for today. It's for Friday of next week. But there's another post office in town that does passports and photos without an appointment. They'll be open all day tomorrow, so give them a try if you need to apply for your passport quickly."

Mark didn't say a word, but she could feel the weight of his anger. It was like a dark cloud all around him.

Once they were back in the truck, Beth broke the silence, "I'm sorry I got the dates wrong, but at least we'll be able to take care of applying for our passports tomorrow."

Mark flatly replied, "We're not going to The Bahamas."

"Mark, let's just do the passports tomorrow. It's not a big deal."

"No, we're not going on a vacation. You should have gotten the date right. If you had gotten it right, we could go on vacation. But you messed it up, so it's your fault we're not going."

The two were quiet for the rest of the ride home. During that time of silence, Beth did a lot of thinking and made the silent decision to keep that appointment.

The following Friday, she secretly went to the passport office, and she applied for her passport without Mark.

When it arrived in the mail several weeks later, she made sure to lay it on the kitchen table where Mark could see it when he came in from work.

And he did. He didn't say a word, but she watched his expression change when he realized she didn't have to have his permission to get her passport.

And for the first time in years, she felt a glimmer of contentment with their relationship.

Jake

"I don't have time to show prospective members around deer camp. I need you to do it," Mark told Beth.

He was president of the local hunting club, and the club was in desperate need of funds to pay the upcoming lease. So, he and some of the other members had advertised heavily in local newspapers. They were getting a lot of response to their ads.

"Mark, I don't really know my way around deer camp that well. I'm not the best person to show people the area."

"I don't have time, Beth. You're going to have to do it."

"What about the vice-president? Can't she take these men up there and show them around?" Beth asked. "She knows everything about camp."

"No, I want you to do it. A man is coming to the house this afternoon so you can show him the hunting territory. He seems really interested in joining," Mark said.

So, Beth did what she was told. It made her uncomfortable to have strange men coming to her home while Mark was at work. And it made her even more uncomfortable to have them get in her truck with her and then drive nine miles into the isolated, wooded countryside to get to deer camp. She showed them around the property to the best of her ability, and some of them paid the expensive dues and joined the club. That was the goal. It all worked out well.

Except for Jake. Something was different with him.

Beth showed him around camp, and he joined. As wife of the club president, and unofficial tour guide, she had given him her phone number.

Which he used.

At first nothing unusual happened. Mark and Beth came across him at camp on occasion during the pre-hunting season when all the members were working on preparing their hunting stands. One day in particular, they came across Jake while he was loading some cumbersome equipment into the bed of his truck. They parked behind him on the gravel road and spoke briefly. Then Jake went back to loading his truck. Beth could see he needed help, so she said something about it to Mark.

"Mark, shouldn't you get out and help him?"

"He can load his truck himself," Mark said.

Beth couldn't stand to sit in the truck and watch him do all that work alone, so she got out and helped him load his gear. Once all of his equipment was loaded, she picked up his 50-pound bag of deer corn and put that in the back of his truck too.

Jake said, "Here, let me get that. That's too heavy for you."

"Oh, I handle these bags of corn all the time. I don't mind loading it for you," she said.

For Beth, this was a moment of helping a fellow human with a menial task.

For Jake, it was the beginning of a fascination with Beth.

He began to flirt with Beth through texts. She didn't say anything to Mark at first. Honestly, she liked the attention. He wasn't an attractive man. And she firmly believed him to be a liar based on some of the things he had told other camp members. She had no actual interest in him. But she enjoyed having the attention, so she allowed the virtual flirting for a few days.

Over a short period of time, Jake became aggressive with the messages he was sending.

"I'll be at camp this afternoon. Meet me there," he said.

"No," she responded. "I'm not meeting you."

"That's what you say, but you'll be there," Jake replied.

"No," she said. "I'm married. You're married. It's not happening."

"You'll be there, and you'll sit straddle of me in my camper and I'll rock your world," he said. "And don't tell me no. It's happening."

After several texts of this nature, she stopped talking to him. She blocked his number. But his texts had been so aggressive, in spite of her repeatedly telling him no, that she was concerned he might show up at her house and assault her while Mark was at work. After all, he knew exactly where she lived. He'd met her there the first day so she could drive alone with him into the woods to show him around.

"Mark, Jake has been flirting with me, so I've blocked his number. If you have any business with him, it will have to be through your phone number," she told her husband.

Mark gave her no response. He just looked at her.

"I also want to start using the parking spot closest to the house. I know you like parking close to the door, but I'm afraid he's going to ambush me when I go out to my truck one morning to go to work."

Mark said nothing.

The next day, Beth parked in the parking spot closest to the door of their home. The place where Mark normally parked.

This parking arrangement went on for weeks.

Mark never said a word. He never asked what was going on. He never asked why Beth was scared. Nothing.

He expressed no concern for his wife's welfare whatsoever.

Falling in Love

Part of the problem in their marriage was that Beth didn't set boundaries. Or maybe she set them, but she didn't enforce them. She wanted to always be a pleasant person, someone who was a joy to be around. She never wanted to nag her husband.

But the relationship was in such bad shape after 25 years, that she started talking to Mark about the issues that needed resolving on a daily basis. She told him the things she, as a woman, needed. She persisted. She wanted the marriage to be right. She wanted him to put in some effort and fix the things she asked him to.

He did the bare minimum. She told him she needed multiple hugs a day, so he increased the number of hugs he was giving her by one hug a day. She needed him to look at her when she spoke to him, so he began pausing his TV shows when she spoke. He started calling her loving names like Sweetie and Princess.

She noticed these small changes and she began to develop feelings of love for him. It surprised her. And it was nice.

"I should tell him I see his efforts," she thought after a few weeks. So, one day she did.

"Mark, I want you to know I see you putting effort into our relationship. I want you to know I notice. I honestly feel like I'm starting to fall in love with you," she softly told him.

He smiled.

And then everything changed.

He never put in an ounce of effort toward their relationship again.

He tossed her crumbs. That's all he ever did was toss her crumbs. Crumbs of affection, crumbs of love, crumbs of attention. Just enough to bait her into continuing to be a good little wife.

"I'm so tired…" she thought. "So very tired."

A Friend in the Fire

"He's not a bad person. Not really. He just does things I don't understand. He thinks differently than I do. That's all. Nothing to be concerned about," she thought.

 She was gentle by nature. And he was… different… but she was sure everything was ok. Their differences were just that – merely differences.

She never understood him. Never understood why he got angry over nothing. Never understood why he gave her the silent treatment when he felt she needed to be punished. Never understood why he was always trying to change her. She never understood why he was the way he was. But it was alright.

"Everyone is different, after all," she thought. "It takes all of us to make the world go 'round."

They were at a party. A handful of friends gathered around a campfire in the woods.

Music playing, drinks being passed around. The fire was hot, perfect. Everyone was having a good time making great memories together.

A line dance song came on, so most of the group stepped a few yards away from the fire and began line dancing at the edge of the firelight.

Beth was dancing, having the time of her life, when she noticed a thick column of sparks shoot up from the fire.

"A log must have shifted," she thought.

And then she looked closer into the fire.

Through the dark of night, gazing into the warm glow of the fire, she realized it wasn't a log that had shifted.

Mark's best friend had stumbled and fallen into the firepit. He was lying in a drunken stupor in the flames. Just lying there. He was too drunk to move. He had fallen into the fire but didn't know what was happening.

She and the others ran to help him.

Everyone but Mark.

While she and the others were trying to roll him out of the fire, Mark was slowly ambling toward the firelight. He was laughing. Laughing and walking so slowly. For him, it was funny that his friend had gotten so drunk that he had fallen into the fire. So, he lifted not a finger to help. He simply stood by and laughed, watching while the rest of them struggled to get his burning, blistering friend out of the flames.

His best friend.

That's the moment. The moment when the differences were no longer simply differences. The moment she realized Mark, her husband, the man she had been living with for 25 years… was demented.

<u>A Time for Lies</u>

It's been five years now, but she remembers it like it was yesterday. It's the day everything changed. It's the day she decided being a good girl didn't work. It's the day she crossed over.

Beth was making the long drive home from her regular job and was enroute to her side gig. She did some small-income work as a sideline. It involved inspecting homes and cars, taking photos, and submitting them to the companies that had requested the information. As she was traveling to her appointment to take photos and measurements of a customer's vehicle, Mark called.

"Are you off work yet?" he asked.

"Yeah, but I'm headed to a client's house right now," she said.

"I need you to meet me at the gas station and jump my truck battery off," he demanded.

"I'm headed to a job right now," she said. "I have an appointment I can't break."

"Beth, I need you to come jumpstart my truck!"

"I will be there as soon as I can. I need to stop and do this inspection first. It's on my route to the gas station anyway, so I'll swing by and make my appointment, and then I'll meet you at the station and jumpstart your truck."

"No, you will not! You will come to the gas station right now!" he shouted.

"Mark, we've been jumpstarting your truck for weeks. You're the one who chooses to drive a truck that won't start instead of just going to the store and buying a battery," she calmly responded.

"Get your butt over here right now! I need to turn off the truck to get gas and I need you to jumpstart it after!"

"I have to keep my appointment," she said. "My customer and I set up this appointment several days ago. He's waiting for me, and I can't be late."

"Fine!" he shouted. "Maybe I can make it home on fumes! Forget about coming to the gas station! But it's all your fault if I end up stranded on the side of the highway with no gas!"

And that was the final straw. She was tired of being yelled at and talked down to. She no longer cared about doing the right thing. She was exhausted.

A woman can only be pushed so far before she breaks.

"From here on out, Beth, old girl, you lie," she told herself.

She'd never lied to him before. She'd always been pure and honest with him.

She was tired.

Tired of being yelled at. Tired of being treated like she had no worth.

She was simply tired.

And, so, she decided to lie if it would keep him from yelling at her.

And lie she did.

Final Chapter – It's Just the Beginning

She'd been married for 25 years and had never once thought of cheating. 25 years of being a loving wife. 25 years of raising children, preparing meals, cleaning the house, mowing the lawn, and working at various jobs.

25 years of being talked to like trash and having her husband's affection withheld from her. 25 years of being told he's not in the mood. 25 years of being told she's not good enough.

In all those 25 years, she never dreamed of stepping outside of the marriage to get her emotional and physical needs met.

Until 25 years and day one.

Sometimes we must release our grip on one thing, so we will have the freedom to take hold of another.

"I've seen you at your lowest lows…I've trudged through the muck with you… holding your hand, sometimes dragging you. I've been to the hard places and watched helplessly as you struggled. Wanting to save you and not sure if I even could…"

Sassy